Distributed Database Architecture

Distributed Database Architecture

Jocelyn O. Padallan

ARCLER
PRESS

www.arclerpress.com

Distributed Database Architecture

Jocelyn O. Padallan

Arcler Press
224 Shoreacres Road
Burlington, ON L7L 2H2
Canada
www.arclerpress.com
Email: orders@arclereducation.com

ISBN: 978-1-77407-710-8 (Hardcover)

ABOUT THE AUTHOR

Jocelyn O. Padallan is Assistant Professor II from Laguna State Polytechnic University, Philippines and she is currently pursuing her Master of Science in Information Technology at Laguna State Polytechnic University San Pablo Campus and has Master of Arts in Education from the same University. She has passion for teaching and has been Instructor and Program Coordinator at Laguna State Polytechnic University

TABLE OF CONTENTS

Glossary .... *xi*

List of Figures .... *xvii*

List of Tables .... *xix*

List of Abbreviations .... *xxi*

Preface .... *xxv*

Chapter 1 Introduction to Distributed Database Systems 1

1.1. Introduction 2

1.2. Characteristics Of Distributed Database Systems 4

1.3. Advantages Of Distributed Database Systems 5

1.4. Disadvantages Of Distributed Database Systems 6

1.5. Problem Areas In Ddbms 7

1.6. Types Of Distributed Database Systems 7

1.7. Database Technology 8

1.8. Data As A Resource 9

1.9. Dbms Architecture 10

1.10. Components Of A Dbms 10

1.11. Approaches To Classify Databases 11

1.12. Hierarchical And Network Dbmss 12

1.13. Database Design And Normalization 13

1.14. Transactions 14

1.15. Concurrency Control Techniques 15

1.16. Integrity Constraints 18

1.17. Integrity Issues In Distributed Databases 19

1.18. Security In Centralized Dbmss 20

1.19. Strong Authentication 22

1.20. Proxy Authentication And Authorization 24

1.21. Database Control 25

1.22. Encryption 26
1.23. Distributed Dbms Reliability 28
1.24. Conclusion 29
References 30

Chapter 2 **Concepts of Relational Databases 31**
2.1. Introduction 32
2.2. Rdbms: Meaning 33
2.3. Structuring Of Relational Databases 35
2.4. The Relational Model 36
2.5. Representing Relations 37
2.6. Relational Vs. Non-Relational Database 40
2.7. Referential Integrity 41
2.8. Benefits Of Relational Databases 47
2.9. Considerations For Selection of Database 49
2.10. The Relational Database of The Future: The Self-Driving Database .. 50
2.11. Conclusion 51
References 52

Chapter 3 **Overview of Computer Networking 53**
3.1. Introduction 54
3.2. Computer Network 54
3.3. Computer Networking 56
3.4. Computer Network Components 61
3.5. Some Protocols For Computer Networking 68
3.6. Types of Network 69
3.7. Internetwork 77
3.8. Conclusion 81
References 82

Chapter 4 **Principles of Distributed Database Systems 85**
4.1. Introduction 86
4.2. Distributed Database Design 89
4.3. Database Integration 95
4.4. Data Security 99
4.5. Types Of Transactions 103

4.6. Workflows 104
4.7. Integrity Constraints In Distributed Databases 105
4.8. Distributed Query Processing 106
4.9. Conclusion 109
References 111

Chapter 5 Distributed Objects Database Management 113
5.1. Database And Database Management System 114
5.2. Database Schemas 115
5.3. Different Kinds of Systems 116
5.4. Distributed Dbms 117
5.5. Object-Oriented Database Management System 123
5.6. Popular Object Databases 129
5.7. Object Management Process, Issues, and Application Examples 133
5.8. Conclusion 142
References 143

Chapter 6 Client or Server Database Architecture 145
6.1. Introduction 146
6.2. Working of Client-Server Architecture 148
6.3. Client And Server Characteristics 150
6.4. Advantages And Drawbacks Of Client-Server Architecture 151
6.5. Client-Server Architecture Types 152
6.6. Concept of Middleware In Client-Server Model 155
6.7. Thin Client/Server Model 157
6.8. Thick Client/Server Model 159
6.9. Services Of Client-Side In C/S Architecture 160
6.10. Services Of Server-Side In C/S Architecture 161
6.11. Remote Procedure Call 163
6.12. Security Of Client-Server Architecture 165
6.13. Conclusion 170
References 172

Chapter 7 Database Management System: A Practical Approach 175
7.1. Introduction 176
7.2. Components of a Database 178

7.3. Database Management System 179
7.4. The Relational Model 188
7.5. Functional Dependency and Normalization 189
7.6. De Normalization 189
7.7. Structured Query Language (SQL) 191
7.8. Query by Example (QBE) 194
7.9. Database Recovery System 195
7.10. Query Processing 196
7.11. Query Optimization 197
7.12. Database Tuning 199
7.13. Data Migration 199
7.14. Conclusion 200
References 201

Chapter 8 Data Warehousing And Data Mining 203
8.1. Introduction 204
8.2. Characteristics of Data Warehouse And Data Mining 206
8.3. Working Process of Data Warehouse 207
8.4. Working Process of Data Mining 208
8.5. Advantages of Data Warehouse And Data Mining 213
8.6. Limitations of Data Warehouse And Data Mining 216
8.7. Olap Vs Oltp 218
8.8. Automatic Clustering Detection 221
8.9. Data Mining With Neural Networks 223
8.10. Conclusion 228
References 229

Index 231

GLOSSARY

A

Asymmetrical Protocol – Client requests for a service and server reply with required data.

Attenuated – Having been reduced in force, effect, or value.

Attributes – A piece of information which determines the properties of a field or tag in a database or a string of characters in a display.

Authentication – The act of proving an assertion, such as the identity of a computer system user. In contrast with identification, the act of indicating a person or thing's identity, authentication is the process of verifying that identity.

B

Bottom-Up Discretization – Split points are continuous values.

Brute Force Attack – Using a different set of passwords again and again until the access to the server is granted.

C

Centralized – Concentrate (control of an activity or organization) under a single authority.

Centralized Server – A single server is present over the network that is responsible for a processing service request to all clients.

Client-Server Architecture – type of distributed database architecture.

Cluster – A small group of people or things.

Connectors – A device for keeping two parts of an electric circuit in contact.

Consistency – Consistent behavior or treatment.

Cryptography – Is the practice and study of techniques for secure communication in the presence of third parties called adversaries.

D

Data Cleaning – Processing of removing inaccurate data present in the storage system.

Data Definition Language – Used to define data elements stored in a database.

Data Description Language – Used to define data structures and database schemas.

Data Discretization – Continuous data values are divided into smaller intervals.

Data Encryption – Converting plain data into cipher data so that information cannot be understood

Data Independence – The type of data transparency that matters for a centralized DBMS.

Data Integration – Data collected from various sources are merged together and stored in a single data warehouse.

Data Manipulation Language – Allows alteration to the data stored in a database.

Data Migration – Transfer of data from one location to another in a database.

Data Transformation – Conversion of data from one form to the other so that different platform can interpret similar data.

Database – A database is an organized collection of data, generally stored and accessed electronically from a computer system. Where databases are more complex they are often developed using formal design and modeling techniques.

Database Management System – A DBMS is a software package designed to define, manipulate, retrieve, and manage data in a database. A DBMS generally manipulates the data itself, the data format, field names, record structure and file structure.

DDBMS – A DDBMS or distributed DBMS is a centralized application that manages a distributed database as if it were all stored on the same computer.

DDL – A data definition or data description language is a syntax similar to a computer programming language for defining data structures, especially database schemas. DDL statements create and modify database objects such as tables, indexes, and users.

Denial of Service Attack – Processing of service is denied from the server-side.

DE Normalization – The process of making the database more efficient for working by inducing redundant data into the tables created after the normalization process.

DML – A data manipulation language (DML) is a computer programming language used for adding (inserting), deleting, and modifying (updating) data in a database.

E

Encapsulation – It is a mechanism of wrapping the data (variables) and code acting on the data (methods) together as a single unit.

Encryption – Encryption is the process of encoding a message or information in such a way that only authorized parties can access it and those who are not authorized cannot.

Entity – A thing with distinct and independent existence.

Expandability – Ability of a computer system to accommodate additions to its capacity or capabilities.

F

Fat Client Thin Server – The client has all the resource and processing requirements which make it less dependent on the server to perform a task.

Field – A field is an area in a fixed or known location in a unit of data such as a record, message header, or computer instruction that has a purpose and usually a fixed size.

Fragmentation -The process or state of breaking or being broken into fragments.

Functionality – The range of operations that can be run on a computer or other electronic system.

H

Hacking – The gaining of unauthorized access to data in a system or computer.

Haphazard – Lacking any obvious principle of organization.

I

Incompatibility – The condition of two things being as different in nature as to be incapable of coexisting.

Inconsistencies – The fact or state of being inconsistent.

Inheritance – It is a mechanism in which one object acquires all the properties and behaviors of a parent object.

K

Kerberos – Is a computer-network authentication protocol that works on the basis of tickets to allow nodes communicating over a non-secure network to prove their identity to one another in a secure manner.

L

Loose Coupling – Data is stored at the original database source.

M

Mapping – Any prescribed way of assigning to each object in one set a particular object in another (or the same) set.

Middleware – Interface between client and server system in a client-server architecture.

O

OLAP – Includes all the analysis process involving the creation, management, and analysis of data.

OLTP – Used for applications that work with individual records and transactions.

P

Polymorphism – It is the ability of a message to be displayed in more than one form.

Primary Key – Used to make relation among different tables created in a database.

Q

Query by Example – Alternate process for SQL top let the non-technical users make changes to the database.

Query Optimization – The queries of the database systems are processed in lesser time and complexity.

R

Redundancy -Refers to information that is expressed more than once.

Reliability – The degree to which the result of a measurement, calculation, or specification can be depended on to be accurate.

Remote Procedure Call – The process by which the client system communicates to a server locating at a remote location.

Retransmission – The action or process of transmitting data, a radio signal, or a broadcast program again or on to another receiver.

S

Schema – Are a set of 'types,' each associated with a set of properties.

Serializability – The classical concurrency scheme. It ensures that a schedule for executing concurrent transactions is equivalent to one that executes the transactions serially in some order. It assumes that all accesses to the database are done using read and write operations.

Server – A computer or computer program which manages access to a centralized resource or service in a network

Service Encapsulation – The client is only required to request a service and wait for the required data; they are not provided with the information about the location of data and how it is being accessed.

Structured Query Language – Used to run queries in a database for addition, deletion, and manipulation of data.

T

Technology – The sum of techniques, skills, methods, and processes used in the production of goods or services or in the accomplishment of objectives, such as scientific investigation.

Thin Client Fat Server -the client is fully dependent on the server to complete a task.

Tight Coupling – Collected data from various sources is stored at a single physical location.

Top-Down Discretization – Initial points are used for attribute range splitting.

Transaction Management – The processes involved in the architecture from client to server and client are managed using a transaction management system.

Troubleshooting – Trace and correct faults in a mechanical or electronic system.

Tuples – A finite ordered list of elements.

LIST OF FIGURES

Figure 1.1. Advantages of database management systems

Figure 1.2. Disadvantages of database management systems

Figure 1.3. Database technology

Figure 1.4. Hierarchical database

Figure 1.5. Concurrency control techniques

Figure 1.6. Integrity constraints

Figure 1.7. Integrity issues in distributed databases

Figure 2.1. An example of a relational database model

Figure 2.2. Explanation for tuple, attribute, and relation

Figure 2.3. Non-relational database

Figure 2.4. Benefits of relational database management

Figure 3.1. Representation of computer network

Figure 3.2. Representation of network topology

Figure 3.3. The various components of computer network

Figure 3.4. The network operating system provides multiple services

Figure 4.1. Different types of fragmentation

Figure 4.2. Data security helps in protecting the data, such as those available in the database

Figure 4.3. Different types of transactions

Figure 4.4. Distributed query processing

Figure 5.1. ANSI-SPARC DB model

Figure 5.2. Overall architecture Of ODBMS

Figure 5.3. Schema integration

Figure 5.4. Interoperability using CORBA

Figure 6.1. Client-server architecture

Figure 6.2. Three tier client-server architecture

Figure 6.3. Thin client-server architecture

Figure 6.4. Thick client-server architecture

Figure 6.5. Symmetric encryption

Figure 7.1. Database management system
Figure 7.2. SQL for database
Figure 7.3. Disadvantages of data base system
Figure 7.4. DBMS transaction management
Figure 7.5. Process for database recovery
Figure 8.1. Data warehouse
Figure 8.2. Aspects of data mining
Figure 8.3. The online transaction processing system
Figure 8.4. Online analytical processing system
Figure 8.5. Feed forward neural network

LIST OF TABLES

Table 6.1. System installation life cycle

Table 7.1. Functional query categories

Table 8.1. Functions and models of neural network

LIST OF ABBREVIATIONS

3NF	3 normal form
ACL	access control list
ADTs	abstract data types
AI	artificial intelligence
ANSI	American National Standards Institute
ARPANET	Advanced Research Projects Agency Network
ATM	automated teller machine
C/S system	client/server system
CAN	campus area network
DAC	discretionary access control
DARPA	Defense Advanced Research Projects Agency
DBA	database administrator
DBMS	database management system
DCE	distributed computing environment
DDBMS	distributed database management system
DDL	data definition language
DES	data encryption standard
DM	data mining
DML	data manipulation language
DoD	department of defense
DoS	denial of service
DSVM	direct shared virtual memory
DT	database tuning
DVD-ROM	digital versatile disc-read only memory
DW	data warehouse
EAI	enterprise application integration
EII	enterprise information integration

EPN	enterprise private network
E-R	entity-relationship
ETL	extract-transform load
GAV	global-as-view
GLAV	global-local-as-view
HAN	home area network
ICA	independent architecture of computing
IDL	interface definition language
IP	internet protocol
JDBC	java database connectivity
JSON	java script object notation
LAN	local area network
LAV	local-as-view
LCSs	local conceptual schemas
LFU	less frequently used
LRU	least recently used
MAN	metropolitan area network
MDBMS	multi-database management systems
MFU	most frequently used
MOD	multimedia film-on-demand
NIC	network interface controller
NoSQL	not only SQL
NPL	national physical laboratory
ODBC	open database connectivity
ODBMS	object database management systems
ODBPP	object database
ODMG	object data management group
OLAP	online analytical processing
OLE	object linking and embedding
OLTP	on-line transaction processing
OMP	object management process
OODB	object-oriented database
OODBMS	object-oriented database management system
OOPL	object-oriented programming language

ORB	object request broker
ORD	object-relational database
ORDBMS	object-relational database management systems
ORM	object relational mapping
OSF	open software foundation
OSI	open system interconnection
P2P	peer-to-peer
PAN	personal area network
PC	personal computer
QBE	query by example
RADIUS	remote authentication dial-in user service
RCA	remote caching architecture
RDBMS	relational database management system
RDP	remote desktop protocol
RM	relational model
RPCs	remote procedure calls
SAN	storage-area network
SILC	system implementation life cycle
S-LRU	size-based LRU
SQL	structured query language
SSL	secure sockets layer
T S	top secret
TCP	transmission control protocol
UDP	user datagram protocol
VPN	virtual private network
WAN	wide area network
Wi-Fi	wireless fidelity
WLAN	wireless local area network

PREFACE

Data is the core of all the information related operations and activities that are taking place around the world in current times. It has the highest significance in the terms of commodities in the world and it is rising by every passing day.

The businesses in the market are making use of as much information and data is available to them as possible so that they can make well-informed decisions and reduce the unnecessary risks involved in the markets.

The significance of data has been highlighted by many prominent nations and leaders across the world too and it is universally accepted that data is the most important commodity in the world at the moment. Data has a major role to play in generating and running employment across the globe.

The data needs to be stored and manipulated as and when desired, bound by the ethical and moral clauses. There are various kinds of data management systems and storage options that decide how data will be manipulated and the developers and analysts make use of the various kinds of systems to carry out their tasks on data.

This book informs the readers about the various kinds of database management systems and explains to them the structure in which the databases are architecture. The book explains the readers the meaning of database systems and throws light on the distributed database architecture.

The readers are well informed about the advantages of distributed database systems, the types of distributed database systems, the manner in which they are architecture, the significance of relational database systems, and their applications.

The book also throws light on the subject of computer networking making the people aware about the various kinds of networks and other aspects of networking. The book makes the readers aware about the significance of integrity in data systems and explains to them the ways in which they can ensure integrity in the various data structures.

The readers are further informed about the distributed objects database systems as the chapter goes on to shed light on the processes related to the object management and more. The book also explains the readers about the client or server-based data structures, by also taking them through each and every aspect of such data systems.

The book then discusses about the database management systems and discusses all the limitations, disadvantages, benefits, functions, characteristics, and the future of database management systems. It explains the readers the concepts that are related to the database management systems.

The readers are also informed about the process of mining the data and data warehousing. They are further informed about the ways in which data mining is related to the data structures and told about the working process of data mining.

I hope that the readers find the book relatable to their interests and that this book is able to provide them with solid knowledge of the data structures and their architecture. I also hope that the book can explain the applications of data systems to the readers and that it can help them out with any doubts on the concepts of data structures and their real-time applications.

CHAPTER 1

Introduction to Distributed Database Systems

CONTENTS

1.1. Introduction 2
1.2. Characteristics Of Distributed Database Systems 4
1.3. Advantages Of Distributed Database Systems 5
1.4. Disadvantages Of Distributed Database Systems 6
1.5. Problem Areas In Ddbms 7
1.6. Types Of Distributed Database Systems 7
1.7. Database Technology 8
1.8. Data As A Resource 9
1.9. Dbms Architecture 10
1.10. Components Of A Dbms 10
1.11. Approaches To Classify Databases 11
1.12. Hierarchical And Network Dbmss 12
1.13. Database Design And Normalization 13
1.14. Transactions 14
1.15. Concurrency Control Techniques 15
1.16. Integrity Constraints 18
1.17. Integrity Issues In Distributed Databases 19
1.18. Security In Centralized Dbmss 20
1.19. Strong Authentication 22
1.20. Proxy Authentication And Authorization 24
1.21. Database Control 25
1.22. Encryption 26
1.23. Distributed Dbms Reliability 28
1.24. Conclusion 29
References 30

A database that is not limited to one system and which is spread over different sites, i.e., on multiple computers or over a network of computers. Physical components are not being got shared by a distributed database system which is located on various sites.

There are various types of database systems, which perform different functions accordingly. Information in database technologies enables users to easily and intuitively go back and find details they are searching for because database technologies take information and store, organize, and process it in a way, which enables users to easily organize and manipulate it.

Database technologies are shareable in two ways and it also comes in all shapes and sizes, from complex to simple, large to small. Each data can be used simultaneously by different users as the same data may have multiple representations in different sets of records. So, this makes data a shareable resource.

1.1. INTRODUCTION

At present, some engineers are facing challenges because of innovations for the information system, as computing is becoming difficult with time. All the advancement is made in methodologies, software, and hardware with the change in technology. New ideas from the researcher bring the demand from the user population for their exploitation.

Along with the new announcements of products, the speed of action will be increased and the size of stores available will also increase. There is a continuous demand for performance, flexibility, and more functionality. Sometimes there are applications which are not relevant to their operations, which means some time user is also not aware of the operations.

An engineer designing a new information system for linking the solutions offered by the technologist to the needs of user applications. Sometimes engineers try to stretch the life of the old system to meet the needs of the user application, as it will be cost-effective. A distributed information system is the one in which solutions are becoming more viable.

A communications network is the link between the distributed information systems. The main concern of this system is to manage data stored in computing facilities at many nodes. In the mid-1970s, a system aimed at the management of distributed databases for the first serious discussion. At the end of that decade schemes of architecture started to appear.

Organizations like health service networks, industrial corporations, or banks having large data. So, a large database manages data that is relevant to the operations. The original dream was that all data access could be integrated using a kit of database tool and it is only done if the data is collected into a single reservoir. Data description languages, data manipulation languages (DML), constraint checkers, very high-level languages are some of the examples.

Many enterprises found that the package was satisfactory to some extent for a reasonable number of users, after some experience with the database approach. Owners found that they have lost control over the data collections. They also thought they were no longer stored at their workplaces. These data collections were used for dynamic tailoring of data structures and details. This was done to fit the needs of individuals which was almost impossible.

Over 90% of input and output data operations are local as per the experience shown. Most of the access is to local data only. Users feel frustration can be expected with the growth of an organization, as they feel whether the data will remain centralized or not. De facto decentralization opted by many organizations users by doing vote by their feet for acquiring departmental database systems.

After this difficulty began to establish in maintaining consistency between the central system and local system. Transferring data between central and local system is also difficult because of operational difficulties. For example, this was done in some cases by keying in data from reports. Formal decentralization of databases and database functions facing the pressure.

Due to difficulties in capacity planning and maintenance problems, there is a rise in evolutionary forces for distribution for security reasons. Data processing at various locations is more desirable as it is done for backup purposes. Maintaining a large file is more difficult than maintaining a partition of the file. So, dividing large files into a small partition is more desirable for maintenance as it can be carried out in isolation from other partitions.

If there will be no data distribution than the cases related to disk overloads will arise, were multiple computer complexes are needed. And similar issues will be there if the connections between devices are not up to scratch up. So, there is a very good technical reason for distributing data. Technical pressure to decentralize has been around for some time. The power of a computer is proportional to the square of its cost.

1.2. CHARACTERISTICS OF DISTRIBUTED DATABASE SYSTEMS

- **Durability:** This processing of the transaction is committed towards the successful completion of the transaction and it is also prepared for subsequent failures.
- **Isolation:** In this property of transaction means execution which states that until the first transaction completes its execution, the effects of one transaction on the database are isolated from other transactions.
- **One Copy Equivalence:** The values of all copies of a logical data item should be identical when the transaction that updates that item terminates is known as the Replica control policy.
- **Query Optimization:** Among the set of alternatives, there will be the best execution of the given query.
- **Query Processing:** Translation of declarative query into low-level data manipulation operations.
- **Serializability:** The effect of some serial execution of transactions should be equivalent to the concurrent execution of a set of transactions as the concurrency control correctness criterion requires that.
- **Transaction:** Against the database, there is a unit of consistent and atomic execution.
- **Transparency:** To distributed systems, there is an extension of data independence by hiding the distribution, fragmentation, and replication of data from the users.
- **Two-Phase Commit:** A transaction is terminated the same way at every site where it executes. Two rounds of messages are exchanged during this process and the name comes from the fact that.

1.3. ADVANTAGES OF DISTRIBUTED DATABASE SYSTEMS

1.3.1. Improvement in Performance

Data may be stored at several sites that are retrieved by a transaction. It also makes it possible to execute the transaction in parallel. Significantly improved in performance is because of using several resources in parallel (Figure 1.1).

1.3.2. Improvement in Reliability/Availability

If data exist at more than one site that means data is replicated. Some sites become inaccessible because of the failure of a communication line or a crash of one of the sites and it does not necessarily make the data impossible to reach. Moreover, the Total system will not get effected or the failures of communication or system crashes do not cause the total system not operable and distributed DBMS can still provide limited service.

1.3.3. Economics

Applications related to data may be much more economical, in terms of communication costs, to partition the application and do the processing at each site, if the data is geographically distributed. The cost of having an equivalent power of a single mainframe is more whereas the cost of having smaller computing powers at each site is much less.

1.3.4. Expandability

By adding processing and storage power to the existing network expansion can be easily achieved. Significant changes are still possible and it may not be possible to have a linear improvement in power.

1.3.5. Shareability

It is usually impossible to share data and resources if the information is not distributed. A distributed database makes this sharing feasible.

1.3.6. Security

In a central location security can be easily controlled with the DBMS enforcing the rules. Network is involved in which it has its security requirements and security control becomes very complicated in a distributed database system.

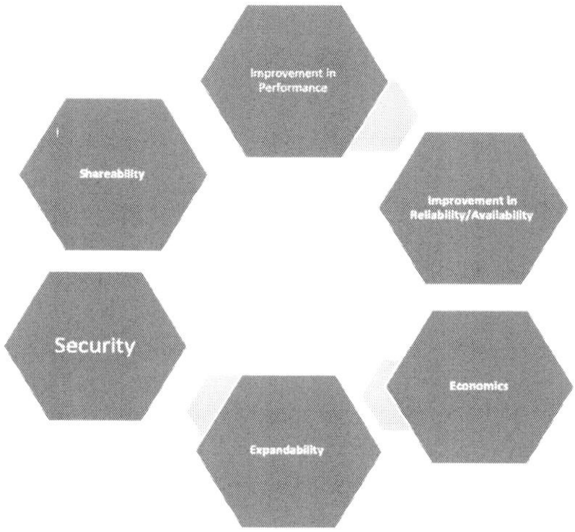

Figure 1.1: Advantages of database management systems.

1.4. DISADVANTAGES OF DISTRIBUTED DATABASE SYSTEMS

- **Complexity:** To set up and maintain a distributed database is more complicated as compared to the central database system.
- **Security:** Central system leading to security threats as compared to there are many remote entry points to the system.
- **Data Integrity**: data need to be carefully placed to make the system as efficient as possible in distributed database systems and in a distributed system it is very difficult to make sure that data and indexes are not corrupted (Figure 1.2).

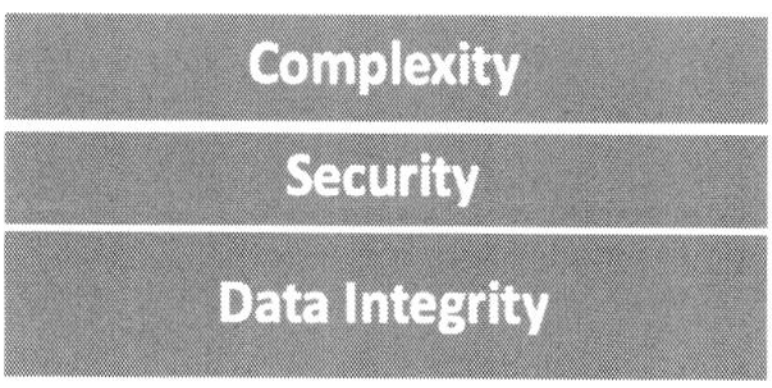

Figure 1.2: Disadvantages of database management systems.

1.5. PROBLEM AREAS IN DDBMS

- **Distributed Database Design**: The separation of the database into partitions called fragments, and distribution, the optimum distribution of fragment is the two fundamentals to minimize the cost of data storage and transaction processing and how to the fragment distribute the database and application program. The two fundamental design issues are fragmentation.
- **Query Processing**: Executing every query over the network in the most cost-effective way but the problem is how to decide a strategy for it. Converting queries into a series of data manipulation operations. Query processing deals with designing algorithms that analyze queries.
- **Distributed Concurrency Control**: When multiple transaction is executing concurrently on a site then it means that it indicates to maintain the integrity of the database.
- **Directory Management**: For the entire database, it indicates how to manage meta-data (Data about Data).
- **Reliability**: To detect failures should ensure the consistency of the database and because of consistency only they recover from them. Various sites become either inoperable or inaccessible when a failure occurs, and the databases at the operational sites remain consistent and up to date.

1.6. TYPES OF DISTRIBUTED DATABASE SYSTEMS

Distributed Database Systems are broadly classified into two types

- **Homogeneous Distributed System**: The data is distributed but all servers run the same Database Management System (DBMS) software and this done only in Homogenous distributed database system,
- **Heterogeneous Distributed System**: Different sites run under the control of different DBMSs in Heterogeneous distributed databases, to enable access to data from multiple sites these databases are connected somehow.

1.7. DATABASE TECHNOLOGY

At the end of the 1960s DBMS first emerged in the marketplace. And today DBMS is sufficiently mature which motivates virtually all information systems today. Database is defined as an integrated collection of shared data and a reservoir of data. The main DBMS is to provide powerful tools for managing the database (Figure 1.3).

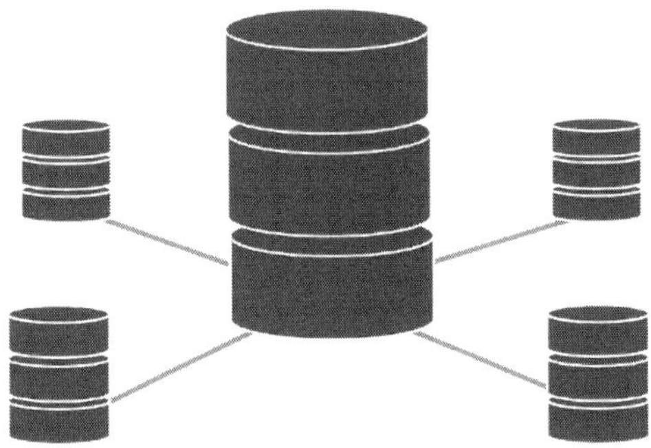

Figure 1.3: Database technology.

Source: Image by Pixabay.

1.7.1. Functions of DBMS

- Physical data structures maintenance.
- Storage retrieval for languages
- Recovery and backup of data
- It also facilitates the maintenance of metadata.
- Independence of data
- Designing and maintenance of database

1.7.2. Types of Database Technologies

- **Engineered Database Systems:** Putting the most efficient hardware together and optimizing the software to run the oracle database at its peak instead of users building a database from scratch. For example, the system moves query processing directly into storage to make analytics run much faster.

- **In-Memory Database:** in-memory database systems are the systems that primarily rely on main memory. It provides more fast and predictable performance than disk. It can also maintain data in the event of power failure.
- **Big Data Linked to Existing Data:** Companies usually generate big data from the internet or tracking web click streams data for customer trends. But today it is said that big companies already having data.
- **Complete Data Protection:** Data protection is a balancing act between the need to protect data and the need to access protected data. Each data requires different forms of protection.
- **Container Databases:** Container database manages multiple data as a pluggable database. Each pluggable database thinks it has own private resources, but it's sharing them as part of one container, which makes managing and stacking easier.
- **Cloud-Based Database**: It is the database with the latest security features and performance. It also helps in managing huge applications, so developers or testing teams want a database environment up.

1.8. DATA AS A RESOURCE

Database technology is very useful for all the companies having large data. It offers a conventional file system having the ability to integrate data about different applications within an organization. It also enabled the sharing of corporate data resources. Incompatibility, redundancy, and data dependency are some of the problems which are overcome by database technology which were inherent in traditional file-based systems, while at the same time providing reliability, integrity, and security.

Database technology offers a powerful tool for the management of corporate data resources. Before management recognized the vital role that the data managed by these systems played in the efficiency and indeed profitability of the organization, the computer-based information system had been in regular use in many organizations.

Information systems provide decision support to management for strategic planning, so it is not simply used as data management tools that balance the accounts, process orders, print the pay checks and so on. Data came to be regarded as a resource that is just as critical as plant and personnel. The practical approach is provided by database technology to control and manage the data resource.

1.9. DBMS ARCHITECTURE

Today available DBMSs are based on ANSI-SPARC architecture. It divides the system into three levels - internal, conceptual, and external. The conceptual level does not take into account how individual applications will view the data or how it is stored. Its production is the first phase of database design. The conception view is defined in the conceptual schema.

Users view data through an external schema which is defined at an external level. Users also include application programmers. A widow is provided by the external user on the conception view which allows users to see on those data which are of their interest and protect them from other data. External schemas be it any number can overlap with each other and can also be defined.

1.9.1. Types of Database Architecture

1 **Tier Architecture**: In this database is directly available to the user and the user can directly sit on DBMS and use it. It does not provide any hand tool for end-user and changes here will be soon on the direct database. It is also used for the development of the local application, where programmers can directly communicate with the database for the quick response.

2 **Tier Architecture**: In this database applications on the client can directly communicate with the database at the server-side. The server side is responsible to provide functionalities, such as query processing and transaction management. On this client-side establish a connection with the server-side.

1.10. COMPONENTS OF A DBMS

The data dictionary or catalog lies in the system of the heart of DBMS. Along with all other components of the system interact virtually. Catalog contains all the meta-data for the system. It is the description of all the data items. The query processor is responsible for retrieve and update data in the database and it is responsible for accepting commands from end-user.

Interpretation of these requests is done based on information stored in a catalogue. After interpretation translates them into physical data access request which can be passed to the operating system for processing. Application programs are written in 3GLs using embedded database languages generally go through a preprocessor which converts the database commands into procedure calls before passing the program on to the 3GL language compilers.

Transaction is a process of updating and retrieving user data. In a DBMS, various users can access the services simultaneously. Thus, it has the function of performing various transactions at once. In a single processor, it is not possible to perform various transactions at a single instance due to limited processing power and resource availability.

However, multiple transactions can be performed in a multiprogramming environment where the processors are not limited in computing power thus have the proper resources to provide services to various users at a single time. This is done by providing a CPU from one user to the other. This process is done with the help of a priority-based scheduling process in which the user task is given priority and based on that the user programs are completed.

In a database environment, the transactional interleaving is a complex procedure to be followed. Thus, in the case of distributed architecture interleaving and parallel processing can be done simultaneously. In comparison to the traditional file system processing, this technique provides enhanced backup and recovery services.

Like many systems, this system is also not fully reliable but it has enhanced the capability of failure tolerance. The database failures can be tolerated by the system and for that, they are required to be designed accordingly. There are various causes of failure in a database environment from application program errors to operator error, disk head crashes and power failures.

Thus, the recovery manager performs different actions to deal with these database issues. The database corruption is efficiently dealt by the transaction manger so that the transactions do not coincide with each other.

1.11. APPROACHES TO CLASSIFY DATABASES

DBMSs are generally classified according to how data is represented in the conceptual schema (i.e., the conceptual data model). There are three main approaches:

- Relational;
- Network; and
- Hierarchical.

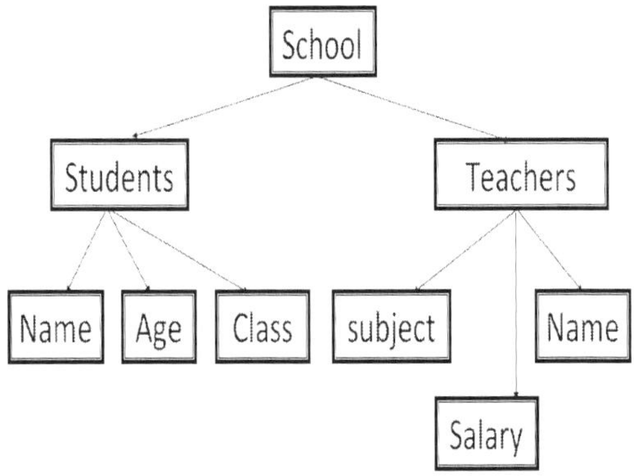

Figure 1.4: Hierarchical database.

Source: Image by Wikipedia.

The main discussion is on the relational system. The most important model is the relational model (RM); therefore, it is used to explain the concepts throughout. Relational database technology is said to be attractive as it is known for its simplicity and it has a sound theoretical basis in mathematical relational theory (Figure 1.4)

Structures known as tables or relations are two dimensional through which data is viewed in a relational database. It supports relations at the conceptual and external levels while describing a DBMS as relational. But at an internal level, there are no restrictions. Tuples mean a variable number of rows in each table and attributes mean a fixed number of columns each table is having.

1.12. HIERARCHICAL AND NETWORK DBMSS

Almost a decade before the relational system, hierarchal, and network systems were developed and commercialized. Their origins in the traditional file processing system are naturally more evident. Both hierarchical and network DBMSs are record-oriented. They process one record at a time. Not like relational DBMS which supports set-oriented processing.

Moreover, the Common domain is the way through which attributes are drawn for relationships in relational DBMSs. Relationships are visible to the user in hierarchical and network systems and the relationship is very clear implemented by pointers. Therefore, hierarchical, and network systems adopt a navigational approach whereas relational systems adopt a declarative approach to database processing.

This also requires to keep the track of current positions in the database and this is not only making the actual writing of programs more difficult. Relational systems are quickly replacing all other DBMSs. Hierarchical and network systems offer considerable advantages in performance can be argued. Though, disks, and CPUs get faster with the maturity of DBMS.

Even for large databases, these disadvantages are being overcome. To illustrate hierarchical and network DBMSs there is a need use a banking database. Information about customers and their accounts and the transactions against those accounts stores in DB. IBMs information management system, IMS is the best-known hierarchical DBMS. It is one of the most widely used DBMSs in the 1970s. In a hierarchical DB, data is stored as a series of trees consisting of a root and zero or more sub-trees.

1.13. DATABASE DESIGN AND NORMALIZATION

Normalization is the process in which parallel development of techniques is the result of the development of relational DB technology. These techniques are developed for good logical design. It is the design of a conceptual schema. Logical DB examines the relationship between them.

This is done because there is a view to grouping them into relations in such a way as to eliminate unnecessary data redundancy and avoid other undesirable features. It also involves taking all the attributes that are to be stored in the DB.

Deign of any software should be headed by the requirements of the software life cycle, so the design of DB should also follow the same. Data items that should be stored in the DB will among other things that identify attributes. To identify the meaning and their relationship to one another. Information about each patient is to be stored, in case of patient DB. Every single information about the patient is to be recorded such as the patient number, name, date of birth, address, sex, and GP.

There is a need to know whether a patient can have more than one address or more than one GP and whether the patient number uniquely identifies a patient or whether it is just the date on which the patient's details were recorded on the DB, to carry out the DB design process.

This information referred to as enterprise rules, as they specify how the data is used by the enterprise being modeled in the DB. And this information can be represented in the form of rules. Some of the rules for patient DB are:

Unique patient number, which means each patient is identified by the single unique number only.

For each patient, there will be only one name, one date of birth, one address, one sex, and one GP.

The maintenance problem is created by redundant data wastes disk space. Changing data is necessary if the data is more than in one place. Data must be changed the same the data is in all locations. If the data is stored only in the customer table like the address of the customer it will be easier to change.

It will be more difficult for the user to investigate the customer table for a customer. It is not necessary to look out for the person who calls the customer. So, this is inconsistency of data that can make data difficult to access because the path will be missing through which data can be found.

Real-world scenarios do not allow for perfect compliance as there are many formal rules and specifications. Additional tables and some customers are required in normalization, to find the cumbersome.

1.14. TRANSACTIONS

Concurrency control is the notion of transaction of the fundamental importance. A transaction is carried out by a single user/application program and defined as a series of actions. A transaction must be treated as an indivisible unit. Transfer of funds from one account to another is an example of a transaction. Consistency of transactions may be violated during transaction execution.

Transform the database from one consistent state to another consistent state. For example, if there is a transfer of funds than the database will be an inconsistent state during the period between the debiting of one account and the crediting of the second account. The database could be inconsistent if the failure occurs during this time. Transactions active at the time of failure should be rolled back, as it is the task of the recovery manager of the DBMS.

Rollback operation is done to restore the database to the state it was in before the start of the transaction and hence a consistent state. Four basic A.C.I.D properties of the transaction are:

- **Atomicity**: An indivisible unit is referred to as a transaction.
- **Consistency**: Consistently transforming the transaction from one consistent state to another consistent state.
- **Independence**: Independently execution of transactions of one another.
- **Durability**: Transactions are permanently recorded in the DB and cannot be undone.

The database environment can be viewed as a series of atomic transactions with non-database processing taking place in between when there is an execution of an application program. The role of the transaction manager is to coordinate database requests on behalf of the transaction and oversee the execution of transactions. Implementation of a strategy is done by the scheduler on the other hand.

His objective is to maximize concurrency without allowing concurrently executing transactions to interfere with one another and so compromise the integrity or consistency of the database. The transaction manager responds to a database request from an application that will depend on the scheduler being used and the transaction manager and scheduler are very closely related.

1.15. CONCURRENCY CONTROL TECHNIQUES

There are three basic concurrency control techniques which allow transactions to execute safely in parallel subject to certain constraints:

- Locking methods;
- Timestamp methods; and
- Optimistic methods.

All these 3 methods have been mainly developed for centralized DBMSs and then extended for the distributed case. Sometime in the future, there may be a conflict with other transactions. Two essential approaches are locking and time stamping in which they cause a delay in the transaction.

Allowing a transaction to proceed unsynchronized and the method based on the premise that conflict is rare is known as an optimistic method. In the end, it only checks for the conflicts when a transaction commit.

An approach that is most widely used to handle concurrency control in DBMSs is known as the locking methods approach. Several variations are there but all share the same fundamental characteristic.

A transaction must claim a read (shared) or write (exclusive) lock on a data item before the execution of the corresponding read or write operation on that data item. Simultaneously on the same data item, it is permissible for more than one transaction to hold read locks.

So, this means read operations cannot conflicts. Therefore, no other transactions can read or update that data item until the transaction holds the write lock on the data item. Lock is continuously held by the transaction until it explicitly releases it. This can be only done when a write lock has been released that the effects of the write operation by that transaction will be made visible to other transactions.

To sum up, at any one time on any one data item there can be any number of read locks. The existence of a single write lock on that data item precludes the existence of other simultaneously held write or read locks on that data item, if a transaction holds a write lock on a data item, then it can downgrade that lock to a read lock, once it has finished updating the item. This will potentially allow greater concurrency

No locks are involved and there can, therefore, be no deadlock. There is quite a difference in the timestamp methods of concurrency control from locking methods. Generally, transactions which make conflicting request wait are involved in locking methods. Along with this on the other side, there is concurrency control 191 no waiting.

Transactions can simply be rolled back and restarted which are involved in a conflict. To order transactions globally in such a way that older transactions, transactions with smaller timestamps, get priority in the event of conflict and this the fundamental goal of times tamping methods.

The last update on that data item was carried out by an older transaction only If a transaction attempts to read or write a data item, then the read or write will only be allowed. Else requesting transactions given a new stamp and it will be restarted.

Assigning should be done to the transactions to prevent them from continually having their commit request denied and this assigning should be done by new timestamps. Transaction with an old timestamp might not be able to commit due to younger transactions having already committed and this is only in the case when there is an absence of new timestamps.

Serializable schedules are the on which are produce by timestamp methods. At the time of successfully committed transactions, serializable schedules are equivalent to the serial schedule defined by the timestamps. Concerning each other timestamps are used to order transactions. A unique timestamp is assigned to each transaction at the time of its launch. So, it is impossible that two transactions can have the same timestamp.

By using the system clock, it can be generated very easily in centralized DBMSs. Therefore, when the transaction is started timestamp of a transaction is simply the value of the system clock. It is said that it is assigned the next value from the transaction counter, which is then incremented when a transaction is launched.

There is a sequence number generator or a simple global counter which operates like a 'take-a ticket' queuing mechanism. Counter can be periodically reset to zero only when there is a need to avoid the generation of very large timestamps.

Based on the premise that conflict is rare and that the best approach is to allow transactions to proceed unimpeded by complex synchronization methods and without any waiting is the optimistic method of concurrency control.

The system only then checks for conflicts when a transaction wishes to commit. A restart of a transaction is only done in the case in which the event of conflict being detected. So, positively allow transactions to proceed as far as possible.

All updates should be made to transaction-local copies of the data to confirm the atomicity of transactions. And all the transactions should only be propagated to the database at commit when no conflicts have been detected. The transaction is rolled back and restarted, in the event of a conflict.

Restarting a transaction involve overheads which is considerable. Redoing the entire transaction is what it effectively means. If it happened very infrequently then it could only be tolerated. It will be the only case in which the majority of transactions will be processed without being subjected to any delays (Figure 1.5).

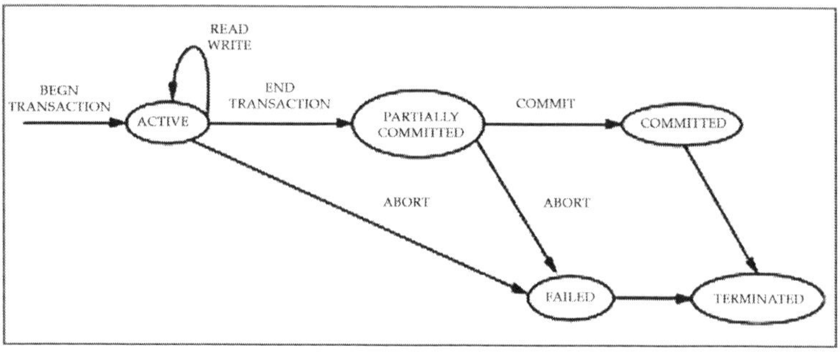

Figure 1.5: Concurrency control techniques.

Source: Image by Gradeup.

1.16. INTEGRITY CONSTRAINTS

There are four types of integrity constraints:

- Domain;
- Relation;
- Referential; and
- Explicit.

Grouping together of the first three and referred to as implicit constraints. They are an integral part of the relational data model. Relation is simply defined by the relation constraints. RDBMSs supports all its attributes. Individual attributes are the ones which defined under the domains and these are not explicitly supported by all RDBMSs (Figure 1.6).

Most vendors of RDBMSs promise to provide support in their next lease, whereas referential integrity constraint is also not universally supported. Specification of explicit constraints supported by few systems like mainly research prototypes and in a limited way. Rules of the real world impose some explicit constraints which are not directly related to the RM itself.

For example, if a person is having a bank account and his credit ratings poor, then he will not be allowed to be overdrawn. To trigger a specific action such explicit constraints can also be used. For example, the order will be produced automatically, if a stock level falls below the reorder level.

Later on, there will be various examples of different kinds of integrity constraints that will be seen. Conceptually, the integrity subsystem of the

DBMS is accountable for enforcing integrity constraints. It has to find out the violations and, in case there is a violation, one should take some appropriate action.

Since there is the absence of failures and assuming correct concurrency control, the only way in which the integrity of a DB can be compromised is as a result of an update operation. Therefore, the integrity subsystem must monitor all the update operations. Data will be updated by various applications in a large multi-user DB environment.

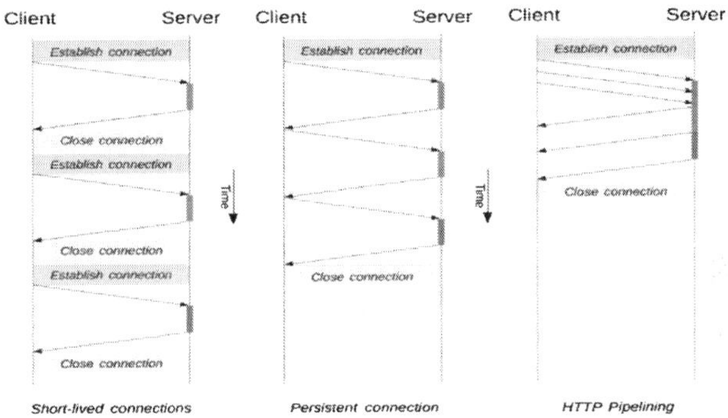

Figure 1.6: Integrity constraints.

Source: Image by Gitlab.

1.17. INTEGRITY ISSUES IN DISTRIBUTED DATABASES

Apart from concurrency control and recovery, it has been observed that very little research has been carried out on integrity issues for distributed databases, particularly for multi databases. Homogeneous distributed databases have been designed 'top-down.' In this case, there is generally no problem. Explicit and implicit integrity constraints can be described at DDB design time and implemented into the integrity subsystems of each of the local DBMSs consistently (Figure 1.7).

Although, it has to be noted that the division into global and local levels in multi databases makes consistent support for integrity constraints much harder. These problems can be divided into three main groups:

- Inconsistencies between local integrity constraints;

- Difficulties in specifying global integrity constraints; and
- Inconsistencies between local and global constraints.

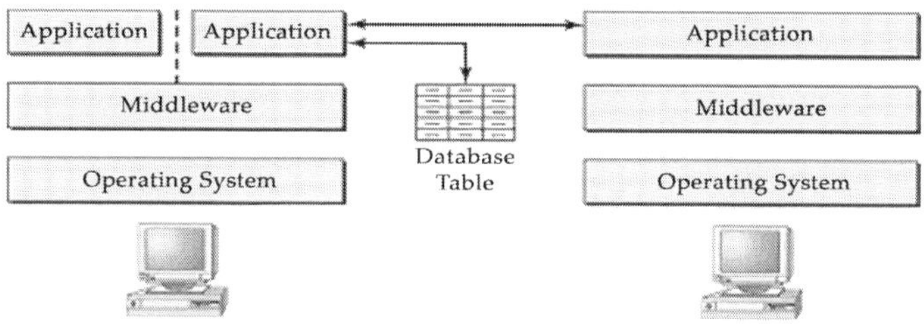

Figure 1.7: Integrity issues in distributed databases.

Source: Image by gitlab.

1.18. SECURITY IN CENTRALIZED DBMSS

In large DBs ensuring the security of data is a difficult task and imposes an access overhead on users of the DB. The installation level of security will depend on data that how valuable or sensitive data is. Like physical security: £1,000,000 would be guarded more carefully than £1. So, it is necessary to consider the level of security to impose on DB. Along with this, there is also a need to consider the implications of a security violation for the organization which owns the data.

If, for example, criminals gained access to a police computer system in which details of surveillance operations and suchlike were stored, the consequences could be serious. The development of secure computer systems has come from military applications these systems are said to be the most advance system. To avoid competitors gaining inside knowledge about the company or to prevent fraud being perpetrated by employees many other organizations also require security.

1.18.1. Security Issues in Distributed Databases

The security of data will ultimately be the responsibility of the local DBMS. This will happen only in the case in which DDB with nodal autonomy. However, there was a time when a remote user has been granted permission to access local data. Ensuring the security of that data is not possible as the local site no longer has any means. This is because such access implies copying the data across the network.

Security of the network must be considered because of issues such as the relative security level of the receiving site. Sending confidential data over an insecure communications link or sending it to an insecure site, so there is no point in a secure site. Four additional security issues that are peculiar to DDBs there will be need to look at in this section. Taking responsibility for its data at its site is assumed by local DBMS.

1.18.2. Identification and Authentication

Knowing the user is the basic security requirement. Before it can determine privileges and access rights an individual must first identify users. Then only individual can audit his or her actions upon the data an individual must know who a user is.

Before users can create a database session, users can be authenticated in several different ways. In database authentication, an individual can define users such that the database performs both identification and authentication of users.

Authentication is performed by the operating system or network service in external authentication, so an individual can define users such way. Secure Sockets Layer (SSL) is an alternative way by which an individual can define users such that they are authenticated. To authorize their access to the database through the enterprise roles enterprise directory can be used for enterprise users.

To connect through a middle-tier server an individual can specify users who are allowed. They assume the identity of the user and allowed to enable specific roles for the user and authentication is given by the middle-tier server. This is known as proxy authentication.

1.18.3. Passwords

Basic forms of authentication are passwords. While establishing a connection to prevent unauthorized use of the database a user must provide the correct password. To connect to a database can be authenticated by using information stored in that database is the only way in which users are attempting. When users are created passwords are assigned. The data dictionary in an encrypted format database can store a user's password. At any time, users can change their passwords.

It is always required that passwords be kept secret because database security systems that are dependent on passwords. But passwords are vulnerable to theft, forgery, and misuse. Several steps can strengthen the basic password feature and provide greater control over database security:

- DBAs can control Password management policy and security officers through user profiles;
- For password complexity, DBA can establish standards, such as minimum password length;
- Passwords should be in words that cannot be easily found in the dictionary. They should not consist of names or birthdates of people;
- Passwords will expire after a certain amount of time. This requires users to change their value periodically. After a certain amount of time reuse of passwords can be prohibited; and
- The server will automatically lock the user's account when a particular user exceeds a designated number of failed login attempts.

1.19. STRONG AUTHENTICATION

Authenticate all members of the network having a central facility (clients to servers, servers to servers, users to both clients and servers). It is one effective way to address the threat of nodes on a network and falsifying their identities. By using two-factor authentication strong authentication can also be established: the combination of something the user has (such as a token card) and something a user knows (such as a PIN).

Some important advantages of Strong authentication:

- There are many choices of authentication mechanism are available, such as smart cards, Kerberos, or the operating system;
- Services like Kerberos and DCE which are known as network authentications services, support single sign-on. This means that users have fewer passwords to remember;
- There may be less administrative overhead to use that mechanism with the database as well. If an individual is already using some external mechanism for authentication; and
- There are a variety of strong authentication methods in this section which describes how that can be used in a distributed environment:

1.19.1. Kerberos and Cyber Safe

Massachusetts Institute of Technology created a trusted third-party authentication system Kerberos. On this free of charge on the internet is provided.

Kerberos enhanced PC security and it relies on shared secrets. Kerberos relies on shared secrets. It provides single sign-on capabilities, centralized password storage, database link authentication and it presumes that the third party is secure. This is done through a Kerberos authentication server, or Cyber safe Active Trust, a commercial Kerberos-based authentication server.

Several benefits are provided by Kerberos Single Sign. The administrative overheads will reduce only with one centralized password. It requires users to remember only one password. It allows controlling network access. It secures against unauthorized access and packet replay employing DES encryption and CRC-32 integrity. Moreover, it allows current user database links. Users connecting with single sign-on through Kerberos can propagate a client's identity to the next database for Kerberos as Kerberos-enabled databases.

The commercial version of Kerberos is Cyber safe. It adds certain extra features and support, including support for the Cyber safe Active Trust server. Cyber safe provides single sign-on and centralizes security. Like Kerberos, it provides a much stronger authentication mechanism, but it is based on passwords.

1.19.2. Radius

As a common communication authentication vendor adopt method The RADIUS protocol (Remote Authentication Dial-In User Service) which is an industry-standard protocol. Between a client, RADIUS provides authorization and accounting. It also provides user authentication, between a client and an authentication server.

All organizations allowing users to access the network remotely as it has been implemented by almost all organizations. Because of its widespread acceptance in the industry, its flexibility, and its ability to centralize all user information to ease and reduce the cost of user administration, so enterprises have standardized on RADIUS. The entire authentication process takes place seamlessly and transparently and it is from the user's perspective,

1.19.3. Token Cards

The two-factor method of authenticating users to the database is provided by token cards. A user must possess the physical card, and must know the password to gain access.

Through several different mechanisms Token cards (SecurID or other RADIUS-compliant cards) can improve ease of use. Some token cards dynamically display one-time passwords that are synchronized with an authentication service.

By contacting the authentication service, the server can verify the password provided by the token card at any given time. Other token cards operate on a challenge-response basis and have a keypad. The user enters a token card is a challenge offered by a server in this case. The user enters and sends to the server is a response provided by the token cards.

1.19.4. Distributed Computing Environment (DCE)

Services that work across multiple systems to provide a distributed environment are the set of integrated network services which is known as Open Software Foundation (OSF). Remote procedure calls (RPCs), directory service, security service, threads, distributed file service, diskless support, and distributed time service are some services that network services include.

Between distributed applications and the operating system/network services, DCE is the middleware. It is based on a client/server model of computing. DCE provides services and tools and by using that, users can create, use, and maintain distributed applications that run across a heterogeneous environment.

1.20. PROXY AUTHENTICATION AND AUTHORIZATION

It is necessary to control the security of middle-tier applications by preserving client identities and privileges through all tiers, and auditing actions taken on behalf of clients in multitier environments, such as a transaction processing monitor.

The only feature that is Proxy authentication that permits to do this. For example, it allows the identity of a user using a web application to be passed through the application to the database server. This has several consequences.

- To validate the credentials of a user by passing them to the database server, in some cases, so in this case, it permits the application.
- To regulate which users can access the database server through a given application, so in this case, it allows the database administrator (DBA).
- To audit actions of the application acting on behalf of a given user, so in this case, it allows the administrator.
- To authenticate and act on behalf of a specific set of users each middle tier can be delegated ability. Along with a specific set of roles, proxy authentication supports a limited trust model for the middle tier server. It also avoids the problem of an all-privileged middle tier.

More privilege to a trusted middle tier than to a less-trusted middle tier is also possible to. Moreover, it is easier to audit the actions of users in a three-tier system, and thus improves accountability because the identity of both middle tier and the user are passed to the database through a lightweight user session.

1.21. DATABASE CONTROL

To provide correct data to authentic users and applications of a database, database control enforcing regulations. All data should conform to the integrity constraints defined in the database to see that correct data is available to users. From unauthorized users, data should be screened away, to maintain the security and privacy of the Database. Primary tasks of the database administrator (DBA) is Database control

Dimensions of database control are:

- Access rights; and
- Integrity constraints.

1.21.1. Access Rights

Rights to create a table, drop a table, add/delete/update tuples in a table or query upon the table are some of the rights which are only privileged to the user given regarding DBMS operations.

It is not feasible to assign individual access rights to users in distributed environments, because there are many tables and a yet larger number of users. So, certain roles are defined by DDBMS. With certain privileges within a database system, a role is constructed.

After defining the different roles, one of the roles will be assigned to an individual user. Even after a hierarchy of roles, roles are defined according to the organization's hierarchy of authority and responsibility.

1.22. ENCRYPTION

To protect information a DBMS can use encryption in certain situations. It is used where the normal security mechanisms of the DBMS are not adequate. For example, stealing of tapes containing some data or tapping of communicating line by an intruder. The DBMS ensures that such stolen data is not intelligible to the intruder by storing and transmitting data in an encrypted form. Therefore, a technique to provide privacy of data is known as encryption

Parameterized by a key is function by which plaintext is transformed. The plaintext is in which the message is encrypted in encryption. Ciphertext is referred to as the output of the encryption process. Over the network, the ciphertext is then transmitted.

Encryption is the process of converting the plaintext too. Decryption is the process of converting ciphertext to the plaintext. At the receiving end, decryption is performed whereas at the transmitting end encryption is performed. The decryption key is needed for the decryption process whereas for the encryption process there is a need of encryption key. An intruder cannot break the ciphertext to plaintext without knowing the decryption key. This process is also called cryptography.

To apply an encryption algorithm is the basic idea behind encryption, which may be a user-specified or DBA-specified encryption key, 'which is kept secret. And, which may' be accessible to the intruder, to the original.

The encrypted version of the data is the output of the algorithm. Which takes the encrypted data and the decryption key as input and then returns the original data is known as decryption algorithm. The decryption algorithm produces gibberish, without the correct decryption key. There must be a relation between the both which must be secret, but encryption and decryption keys may be the same or· different is not clear.

1.22.1. Techniques used for Encryption

Some of the following techniques used for the encryption process:

- Substitution Ciphers; and
- Transposition Ciphers.
- **Substitution Ciphers:** Each letter or group of letters is replaced by another letter or group of letters to mask them and this only done in a substitution cipher. For example, a is replaced with D, b with E, c with F and z with C. In this way *attack* becomes *DWWDFN. An i*ntruder can easily guess the substitution characters, as the substitution ciphers are not much secure because.
- **Transposition Ciphers:** Preserve the order of the plaintext symbols but mask them and this is known as Substitution ciphers. They do not mask them but transposition cipher, in contrast, reorders the letters. A key is used for this process. For example, *iliveinqadian* may be coded as *divienaniqnli.* The substitution ciphers are less secure as compared to transposition ciphers.

1.22.2. Algorithms for the Encryption Process

Some of the commonly used algorithms for the encryption process. These are:

- Data Encryption Standard (DES); and
- Public Key Encryption.
- **Data Encryption Standard (DES)**

  Based on an encryption key it uses both a substitution of characters and a rearrangement of their order. Authorized users must be told the encryption key is the main weakness of this approach. To clever intruders the mechanism for communicating this information is vulnerable.
- Public Key Encryption

  Public-key encryption is another approach to encryption. In recent years it has become increasingly popular. Rivest, Shamir, and Adleman, called RSA is the encryption scheme proposed by them. Every authorized user has a public encryption key that is known to everyone and a private decryption key that is chosen by the user and known only to him or her. They assume encryption and decryption algorithms are to be publicly known.

1.23. DISTRIBUTED DBMS RELIABILITY

"Reliability" and "Availability" of the database have referred to "several times so far without defining these terms precisely." Specifically, these terms were mentioned in combination with data replication. To provide redundancy in system components of building a reliable system is necessary. Distribution of data enhances system reliability.

Though, replication of data items is not enough to make the distributed DBMS reliable or the distribution of the database or the. To exploit this distribution and replication to make operations more reliable, several protocols need to be implemented within the DBMS.

Processing user requests even when the underlying system is unreliable, only a reliable distributed DBMS is one that can continue to. A reliable distributed DBMS should be able to continue executing user requests without violating database consistency, even when components of the DCE fail.

A system that consists of a set of components refers to reliability. The system has a state that changes according to system operates. Responding according to the behavior of the system into all the possible external stimuli is laid out in an authoritative specification of its behavior. Valid behavior of each system state is indicated by the specification. It will be considered as a failure if there is any deviation of a system from the behavior described in the specification.

For example, serializable schedules for the execution of concurrent transactions should be generated in a distributed transaction manager. It will be said as failed if the transaction manager generates a non-serializable schedule. Every failure needs to be tracked to find out the reason for failure. Failures in a system can be there due to deficiencies in the components, design. So, when the components and design put together than it fails.

A reliable system is willfully meeting its specifications. However, an unreliable system may get to an internal state that may not obey its specifications. Eventually, a system cause failure, if further transitions are from this state.

Such internal states are known as erroneous states; the part of the state that is incorrect is known as an error in the system. Any error in the design of a system or error in the internal states of the components of a system is called a fault in the system. Therefore, a fault causes an error that results in a system failure.

1.24. CONCLUSION

In the end, it is concluded that distributed DBMS makes the job of managing the data easy. It allows to store the data at various place, so that one can retrieve the data whenever required. With the implementation of distributed data base management system, the process of sharing of data become viable.

Large companies that have offices located at various place can make the use of distributed data base management system to share the data with one another. In the organization, as there are complexities of tasks and functions, it become necessary to make use of such advance system for smooth operations.

REFERENCES

1. Thakur, D., (n.d.). *What is Data Encryption in DBMS?* [online] Ecomputernotes.com. Available at: http://ecomputernotes.com/database-system/adv-database/data-encryption (accessed on 1 June 2020).
2. Ózsu, M., & Valduriez, P., (2011). *Principles of Distributed Database Systems* (3rd edn., 5th ed.). New York, NY: Springer Science+Business Media, LLC.
3. www.javatpoint.com. (n.d.). *DBMS Architecture – Javatpoint*. [online] Available at: https://www.javatpoint.com/dbms-architecture (accessed on 1 June 2020).
4. Özsu, M., (n.d.). [online] Cs.uwaterloo.ca. Available at: https://cs.uwaterloo.ca/~tozsu/publications/distdb/distdb.pdf (accessed on 1 June 2020).
5. Bell, D., & Grimson, J., (1998). *Distributed Database Systems*. Wokingham, Eng.: Addison-Wesley Pub. Co.

CHAPTER 2

Concepts of Relational Databases

CONTENTS

2.1. Introduction 32
2.2. Rdbms: Meaning 33
2.3. Structuring Of Relational Databases 35
2.4. The Relational Model 36
2.5. Representing Relations 37
2.6. Relational Vs. Non-Relational Database 40
2.7. Referential Integrity 41
2.8. Benefits Of Relational Databases 47
2.9. Considerations For Selection of Database 49
2.10. The Relational Database of The Future: The Self-Driving Database .. 50
2.11. Conclusion 51
References 52

Data is an important part of the information industry in the present times. It requires various technologies and ideas to structure the data for further use. The data has been originally stored in the databases for only reference purposes, but in the last two decades the operability of the data have gained a lot of importance in the information industry.

This has given rise to the databases being modified for the requirements and thus the relational databases have come into the picture. This chapter takes the readers through the various concepts related to the relational databases and explains them to the readers in brief.

2.1. INTRODUCTION

A majority of the issues that come up while implementing the systems are born because of the way the databases are designed, which may not be up to the mark on those occasions. There are many cases in which the systems are required to be changed and updated on a continuous basis as the requirements of the users keep changing from time to time.

This requires a proper plan to be made for the design of the databases. In the databases, a relation is mostly dependent on the manner in which the variables may be related to each other, which may be of many kinds of relations.

One of the most significant ways to apply computers in the professional world is by storing the information and managing it. The way in which the information is organized in the database can have a great impact on the ease by which the information can be accessed and managed. However, it has been seen that the simplest and most apt way to store and use information is to do it in the form of tables.

The relational model (RM) is based on this simple observation which states that the information can be organized into a group of two-dimensional tables which are known as 'relations.' The main aim with which the RM was developed was for the databases which corresponded to the storage of information in the computer systems for long periods of time.

This helped to operate the management systems for databases which were mostly the software that provided the people the ease to store, change, and modify this information. The databases developed at that point of time continue to provide us with the reasons getting a hold of the relational data model.

A relational database may be found to be made up of a large number of relations and the relational database schema that may correspond to them. The main objective with which a relational database is designed is to have a group of schemas for relations that provide the platform for the storage of information, in a manner that there is redundancy in the information and so that the information can be retrieved with ease.

One way in which the schemas may be designed is to have an appropriate normal form. The normal form of designing is followed to make sure that there is not an introduction of various kinds of anomalies and inconsistencies into the databases.

2.2. RDBMS: MEANING

RDBMS is an abbreviated from for Relational Database Management System (RDBMS). The RDBMS is a system in which the information is structured in the form of database tables, fields, and records. All the tables in the RDBMS consist of the rows from the database table.

Each table row in the RDBMS consists of the either one or more fields belonging to database table. The RDBMS makes use of a group of tables to store the data and these tables may be interrelated by some common fields, which appear in the columns in the database tables.

The RDBMS makes use of the various relational operators so that the data stored in those tables can be manipulated by the operators. Most of the RDBMS use SQL as the language for database query and the popular RDBMS may be among MySQL DB2, Oracle, and MS SQL Server.

The RM may be regarded as something that follows a record-based model. The record-based models are the ones based on which the RDBMS structures the data in fixed format records which may be of various kinds.

Each table consists of records of some particular kind and each kind of record indicates towards a particular number of fields or characteristics. The columns belonging to the table may indicate the characteristic of the kinds of records.

The relational data model is one of the most broadly employed kinds of data models and a majority of the database systems that are presently in use, are based on the RM. The RM was one that was designed by a mathematician and scientists at IBM in their research, Dr. E.F. Codd. However, a majority of the DBMS that are currently in use do not the definition of a RDBMS given by Codd, but still they are referred to as RDBMS.

The two main points of focus for Dr. Codd during the research and design on RM included a further reduction of redundancy in data and to make sure that the database systems have integrity in them. The point of origin for the RM of database belong to the paper written by Dr. Codd which had the title "A RM of Data for Large Shared Data Banks" and this paper was authored in 1970.

The concepts included in the paper that apply to the DBMS corresponding to relational databases focus on certain important points. The data structure employed in the relational data model incorporates only the relation so as to represent the entities as well as the relationships that exist between them.

The rows of the relations being used may be referred to as the tuples of the relation and the columns in the database relate to the attributes of the relations. The attributes of the relations may be taken from the set of values that are mostly known as the domains. The domain corresponding to an attribute may be understood as the set of values that can be assumed by the attribute.

Each tuple in a relation can be considered to be a list of components and each relation may be thought to have a fixed arity. Arity can be understood as the number of components that are there in each tuple of the relation.

If viewed from the point of view of the time for which the relational database systems have been there, they may be considered to be new in that regard. The initial database systems used to be based on the models based either on network or hierarchy.

The relational data model has seen itself to be a successful primary model that is widely used for the commercial applications which require huge amounts of data to be processed. This popularity of relational data model has found itself the ways in which it can be applied to other fields outside that of processing of data. These fields include those of Computer Aided Design and similar other work environments.

There are other software as well, in addition to the DBMSs, that can make good use of the information organized in tables and the relational data model makes it easy to design these tables and in developing the data structures that may help the people to access the tables with improved efficiency.

2.2.1. Relations as Set Vs. Relations as Tables

In the RM, as discussed, a relation may be considered a set of tuples. Hence, the order of the listing of the rows of the table has no importance and those rows can be rearranged in any desired manner without having any considerable changes in the value being indicated by the table. It takes place in the same manner as rearranging the values in a given set without having any changes in the value being depicted by the given set.

It is important that the order in which the components of each row appear does not change. This is due to the fact that different columns are named in different ways and each component of the table must be able to represent the item belonging to a kind which is given in the header of the column they appear in.

However, the RM permits the users to permute the manner in which the columns appear along with the name of their headers and still keep the relations same, without having any changes in the value of the relations.

This aspect that is depicted by the database relations is quite different from the relations in the set-theory. But it is very rare to find the columns of the table being reordered, which makes it sensible to keep the terminology of both relations as same. However, in case of any doubt, the 'relations' used in the further text, will have the reference being made only to database structures.

2.3. STRUCTURING OF RELATIONAL DATABASES

The RM of creating databases simply means that the various logical data structures which may be among the data tables, the views and the indexes, must be different and in other space as the structures for physical storage.

The separation thus achieved implies that the various data administrators can handle the physical data storage without having much of an effect on the access that they would have t the data in the form of a logical structure. This can be understood in a way that if one wants to rename a file in the database, it would mean renaming the tables stored in those files.

The point of differences between the physical data storage and the logical data storage can be applied to the database operations as well. The database operations may the actions that have been defined with utmost clarity to change or modify the data accordingly and to manipulate the related structures.

The logical operations given in the database allow the user to have access to the content that the application may need specifically. While, the physical operations decide the manner in which the data may be accessed and then follows it up by carrying out the tasks that have been assigned.

The data must always be accessible and accurate and to ensure this, the relational databases make sure that they follow the integrity rules. The integrity rule may be used for various operations and one among them may be to specify that there must not be any duplicate rows in a table, so that the enormous amount of unwanted information can be kept away from entering the database.

2.4. THE RELATIONAL MODEL

At the time when the databases were coming into the picture, all the applications used to have the data stored in a unique form of its own. If any developer desired to use that data to build an application, it required them a lot to know about the data structure so that they could find the data that was required by them.

This made these kind of data structures inefficient and difficult to manage and maintain. This also made it hard for them to be optimized so that they could deliver a good performance in their application. Hence it was needed that the relational databases be designed so that the issue arising out of the presence of different kinds of data structures could be managed.

The relational data model came to provide a standardized form in which the data could be represented and the queries for data could be made. These queries could be further used by the applications (Figure 2.1).

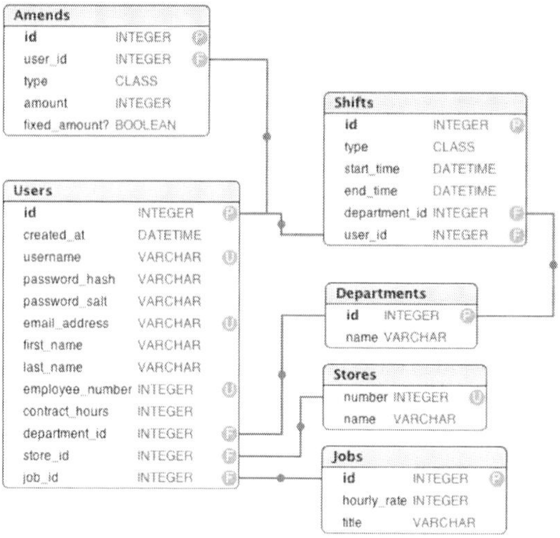

Figure 2.1: An example of a relational database model.

Source: image from Flickr.

It was a well-accepted fact from the beginning that the main characteristics of the relational database was its ability to be represented in the form of tables as they were efficient and flexible in the manner they stored and provided the access to information in a structured form.

As the RMs started to be utilize more, the developers started to make use of the structured query language (SQL) for the querying and writing of data in the database. For quite a lot of years now, the SQL has been used quite broadly as a language for the queries regarding the database.

Taking relational algebra as the basis, the SQL enables the developers with a mathematical language that is internally consistent, which makes it easy for the developers to improve the manner in which the queries to the database are performing, while on the other hand, the other approaches for data structures must define queries individually.

2.5. REPRESENTING RELATIONS

In the form of sets, there are a lot of ways in which relations can be represented by data structures. A table may be considered as a form in which the rows represent the structures and the column names representing the fields. For instance, the tuples in a relation may be given as structures of the type:

- struct CSG {
- char Course [5];
- intStudentId;
- char Grade [2];
- };

The table can itself be represented in various ways and some of which may include:

- An array of structures of the given type
- A list of structures of the given type that is linked together and also has next field so that the cells of the list can be linked together.

In addition to this, one or more attributes can be identified as the domain of the relation and the attributes that remain after this can be considered as the 'range' of the relation. After this, the relation can be stored in the hash tables as per the designated order for the various kinds of binary relations (Figure 2.2).

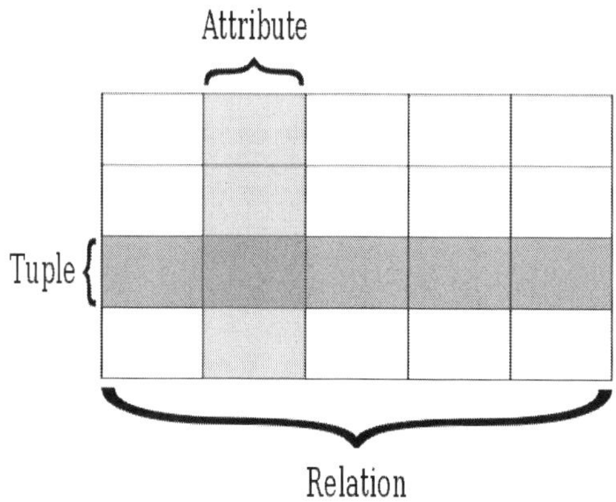

Figure 2.2: Explanation for tuple, attribute, and relation.

Source: Wikimedia Commons.

2.5.1. Primary Storage Structures for Relations

There are some operations which can be speeded up by storing the pairs as per the domain values that they may have given below are some structures in which a relation may be represented.

- One can use a binary search tree, that has a "less than" relation on the domain values so that the placement of tuples can be done in a proper way. It can be helpful in enabling the operations in which the value of a domain is properly specified;
- An array can be used as a vector with certain characteristics, which has domain values as in the form of array index;
- User can employ a hash table which is used to hash the values in order to find the buckets; and
- However, a linked list cannot be used as it does not enable operations of any kind even though in theory a linked list of tuples is a general probable structure.

The same kind of structures may be found to operate when the relation is not binary. The users may have a particular combination of k attributes, that can be used in place of a single attribute. The k attributes are generally known as the domain attributes. They are commonly referred to just as 'domain' when the users may feel that they are clearly referring to a set of attributes.

In such cases, the domain values are k tuples which have one component for each of the attributes of the domain. All the attributes barring the domain attributes are known as the range attributes. The values corresponding to the range may also have number of components, wherein there is one component for each attribute in the range.

Generally, the users are required to choose the attributes that they want for the domain. The simplest scenario to choose the attributes takes place when there is a small number of attributes or only a single attribute which acts as a key one for the relation. In such case it is very common to pick the key attribute to serve as the domain and the other attributes as the range.

However, there might be cases when there is no key attribute except the set of all attributes, which may not be that useful. In such case the users may select any attribute they wish to, as the domain. For instance, there may be some general operations that the users may be expected to perform on the relation. In this, the users may be expected to choose and attribute for the domain that can be expected to specified quite often.

Once the users have chosen a domain, they can choose any one of the four data structures which may just have been given names for the representation of the relation. The users may even select another structure. However, it is very usual to pick a hash table that is dependent on the domain values which may be represented as the index.

The structure that has been picked may be considered to be the primary index structure corresponding to the relation. The term 'primary' has been used to point to the fact that the place at which the tuples are located is decided by this structure.

An index may be regarded as a data structure which has the primary motive of finding the tuples by a given value which may correspond to a component or even more among the desired tuples. There are secondary indexes too that have the feature of answering the queries but do not take part in locating the data.

2.5.2. Choosing Primary Index

Most often it is quite useful to have a key for a scheme related to relation as the domain belonging to a function and the other attributes represent the range. After this the relation can be implemented in a manner similar to that of a function, characterized by the use of index as a hash table and the hash function dependent on the key attributes.

But in case that the most common kind of query lays down the values for an attribute or a set of attributes that are not related to the formation of a key, the users may go for the concerned set of attributes and treat it as the domain, while they treat other attributes as the range.

Then the users may treat and use this relation as a binary relation such as aby a hash table. However, there is a problem that the manner in which the tuples are divided into the buckets, may not be as even as it may have been if the domain were treated as a key.

The most effective influence over the speed that corresponds to the execution of typical queries, is found be that of the choice of domain which has to be made for the primary index structures.

2.6. RELATIONAL VS. NON-RELATIONAL DATABASE

There are various relational databases like MySQL, PstgreSQL, and others that are mainly used to represent and store data in the form of tables and rows. The main theory they are based on is that of algebraic set theory which is commonly known as relational algebra.

There are some non-relational databases as well such as that of MongoDB, which may be found to represent the data in the form of groups of java script object notation (JSON) documents. The import utility in Mongo is designed to import JSON, CSV, and TSV formats of the files. The targets of data corresponding to the queries in Mongo are given as BSON, which is a short form for Binary JSON.

The main language that the relational database uses is that of SQL. This makes these databases a suitable option for operating several kinds of transactions related management activities.

The manner in which a relational database is structured makes a case for the users to link the information available in different tables by the use of the foreign keys, which are also known as indexes and are used to determine smallest of data that is present in the table uniquely.

The other tables have the possibility to refer to the foreign key so that they can have a link between the pieces of data in the table and pieces that are indicated by the use of the foreign key. Such use of foreign key is quite good for the areas in which there is heavy analysis of data required.

If the user desires to have their query, which may be very complicated, handled by the application, or if they need the management of database transactions or the recurring analysis of the data, the relational database may be a good find to their search.

It is also important that the transactions that are to be focused on by the application are processed with utmost reliability and security, if the number of transactions is too much. For such a case, a relational database such as ACID, is a reliable one, wherein the set of properties involved in the transactions related to the database have a reliable processing and which guarantees a referential integrity (Figure 2.3).

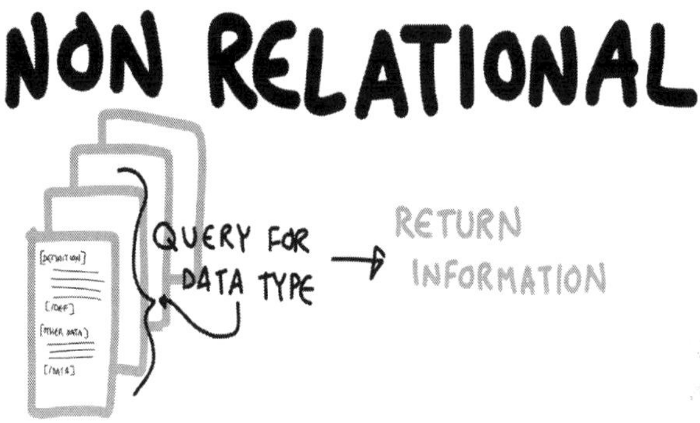

Figure 2.3: Non-relational database.

Source: Wikimedia Commons.

2.7. REFERENTIAL INTEGRITY

When there are multiple database tables involved, referential integrity comes into play. It refers to the situation in which the multiple tables in a database may find a relation among themselves on the basis of the data that is stored in the tables and this relationship is found to be consistent.

The referential integrity in a multiple table database can be kept by employing the functions of addition, deletion, and update of the table on a constant basis. This may be properly illustrated by referring to an example of an app that may be designed to help the victims of human trafficking in finding a safe house for themselves and have access to other important services in real time.

Suppose that there is a city X and it is characterized by two tables namely Trafficking Victim Shelter and Trafficking Shelter Funding. In the table titled Trafficking Shelter there may be two columns namely Shelter ID and the name of the shelter.

the shelters that were not a part of that certain region. This can be done by making use of a SQL SELECT*FROM statement.

The data that exists in the incompatible type systems also needs to be converted to the compatible forms for the ease of readability and comparability in the systems that are characterized by object-oriented programming languages. This process of conversion is known as Object Relational Mapping (ORM).

2.7.1. Non-Relating the Data

Even though the relational databases are a great tool to have, they have certain disadvantages. One of the biggest disadvantages of relational databases is the ORM Impedance Mismatching. This takes place because at the time relational databases were created, the OOP languages could not be considered.

The most suitable way in which this issue can be avoided is by creating a database schema which already has referential integrity as a checkpoint that has been taken care of.

So, at times when the user is operating on relational database that is based on OOP, such as Ruby, they need to give some time on deciding on the manner in which they want to allocate the primary and the foreign keys and the way in which the constraints may be used, which may include the cascade delete or the cascade update function. They also need to think on how they will write their migrations.

However, in case the user is operating on a huge amount of data, which is beyond imagination, the process can get very hard and difficult. In such a case, the probability that an error would occur, as a resultant problem of ORM Impedance Mismatch, goes up.

In such a situation, the user may need to go with a non-relational database. The non-relational database mentioned here is there to store the huge amounts of data, but without the help of a structured mechanism. However, this database does help to link data from the different tables or the buckets to the data from other tables.

A popular example of a non-relational database is that of Mongo. This is a much utilized platform for the MEAN stack developers owing to it being written in the JavaScript. There is a lightweight data interchangeable format commonly known as JSON which is short for JavaScript Object Notation.

In case that the data model that the user is employing turns out to be having complexities, or if there is a case of the user trying to de-normalize the database schema they are working on, it may be best for them to use the non-relational databases such as Mongo. There are various other reasons to use the non-relational database too, which may be given as:

- There may be a need to store arrays in a sterilized form in the JSON objects;
- The records may have to be stored in the same group of data and the records may be having different fields or attributes from each other;
- The user may want to de-normalize the database schema or the user may want to code around the issues that revolve around the performance and horizontal scalability; and
- There may be problems that are pertaining to the schema even before it is formed as the nature of the data model may not be a suitable one.

This concept may further be understood from the following situation. Suppose that a user is developing an application. Now there is a part of the data model that has a lot of complexities and was characterized by a lot of tables, such as that of the example taken above, the safe houses for trafficking victims. This may make the referential integrity too hard to maintain.

Mongo is a database that is accessible with JavaScript. If it is viewed from the perspective of a MEAN stack developer, it would not be recommendable to use any database that cannot be accessed with ease.

One of the most relevant problems that is faced by the MEAN stack developers around the world while using the relational databases is that they have to face unavoidable circumstances of the data being stored in the database in the formats that do not have the ease of access by the frontend people and vice-versa.

However, the non-relational databases are not just restricted to the MEAN stack developers for their utilization. A popular member of the Ruby on Rails community, Steve Klabnik, opted for MongoDB a long time ago. However, there were some of the disadvantages that he had to face as he opted for this kind of database.

The challenges included having problems in restoration of Hackety Hack so that it could be set up for the authentication of the users with the accounts linked to Facebook, Twitter, Github, and LinkedIn. However, the non-relational databases provide some advantages in the form of horizontal scalability, which makes it preferred by several rail developers.

Some other advantages of a non-relational database over that of a relational database are that the database of the user is not at the risk of attacks in the form of SQL injections as the non-relational database do not make use of SQL and are generally lacking a schema.

Some non-relational databases also provide the advantage in terms that once the database is shard, it is done forever. By sharing, it is meant that the data is distributed across various partitions so that various kinds of limitations pertaining to the hardware can be overcome. However, this process gives rise to the problems which may be related to the replication of data.

2.7.2. Detailed Disadvantages of Non-Relational Database

The non-relational databases lack joins which can be found easily in the relational databases. This means that the user has to perform several queries and that they need to join the data together by themselves, manually, within the code they are forming which can be very ugly at times and can end the operations very fast.

As the non-relational database do not consider the operations as transactions automatically as the relational databases do, the user is required to create a transaction manually and after it has been created, they need to very it manually. After this, the users may be required to commit the transaction manually and if it is to be rolled back, that too has to be done manually.

A main thing to consider in the non-relational databases is that the documents may be very complex at times and may be nested, which results in the failure to determine if the operations can be regarded as complete success or failure. This means that while some operations will be successful, the others may fail too.

Hence, it becomes even more important to ask the correct questions and consider the right things so that the data model that the user id going to undertake can be chalked out effectively. This is a key step in deciding the best route that must be taken for the manner in which the application will flow.

This will help determine the correct programming language in which the application must be coded and to determine the database that must be used over some other database, providing the grounds on which this decision will be made.

2.8. BENEFITS OF RELATIONAL DATABASES

The RM is a simple but powerful one that is widely used by the various organizations irrespective of the type and size of the organization and the purpose may incorporate a wide range of needs regarding the information.

The main purposes of using the relational databases are to track the inventories in the organizations, undertake the transactions on the ecommerce platforms and be able to manage a huge amount of customer information that is crucial for the various purposes and findings.

The relational database can be employed for the manipulation of any kind of information which has various data points that can be related to each other and can be managed in a way that is secure, consistent, and based on a certain set of rules. The various advantages that enable the use of relational databases across the globe have been discussed Figure 2.4.

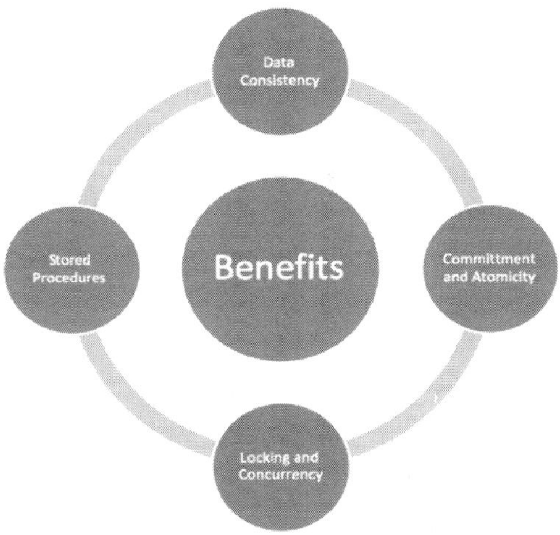

Figure 2.4: Benefits of relational database management.

2.8.1. Data Consistency

The RM of data structures is one of the best ways of maintaining the consistency in the data across various applications and the database copies.

This can be understood from the example of a customer depositing money at an automated teller machine (ATM). In this case, after depositing the money at the ATM, the customer expects that the updated account balance is reflected immediately in the message.

This is the consistency in data that is exceptionally managed by the relational databases, which makes sure that the various copies of the databases are updated consistently with the same data at a given time.

This consistency is a bit difficult to achieve in the other kinds of databases and it gets tougher as the amount of data increase. There are some databases that have been developed in the recent times that can furnish the user with only 'eventual consistency.'

The eventual consistency can be acceptable in some of the cases, as it takes time to catch up with the data and can be used in cases such as to maintain the listings in the product catalogues, but not in critical business operations.

2.8.2. Commitment and Atomicity

The relational databases are capable of handling the various rules and policies that govern a business at all levels and these policies are extremely strict on the commitment, which is about making a permanent change to the database.

In a case of inventory database which is used to keep track of three parts that are always used together, pulling of one part from the inventory must be accompanied by the pulling of other two parts as well. In case that not even one of the parts is available, the others must also not be available. This means that before the database commits anything, all the three parts must be available for review.

In a relational database, it may be taken that it won't commit even for one part until it is confirmed about all the three parts being available for commitment. This capacity of the database focusing on its multifaceted nature is known as the atomicity of the database. Atomicity ensures that the data in the database is accurate and complies with all the rules and policies that the businesses follow.

2.8.3. Stored Procedures and Relational Databases

The access to data involves many actions that repeat themselves. For instance, there may be a simple query that may be required to be repeated several times so that it can produce the results that are desired by the users.

These functions required to access the data nee some kind of code to have access to the database. The developers refrain from working hard repeatedly to write codes every time a new application requires them. The relational databases provide the advantages in these cases where the same codes can be stored in the databases and called for, when needed to be accessed.

2.8.4. Database Locking and Concurrency

There may be various kinds of conflicts that may come up at times when more than one user or applications try to change the data in the database at the same time. Here, the locking and concurrency of the data structures comes into play to reduce the potential conflicts along with assuring the integrity of the data.

The function of locking prevents the other users and applications from having an access to the data during the time when the data is being updated in the database. If in a database, locking is applied to the entire table, it may give rise to a negative impact on the performance of the application.

There are some databases, such as that of the Oracle database, which use locking at the level of records, which makes the other records of the table available for change, making sure that the performance of the application is improved.

The characteristic of concurrency refers to the management of different activities when more than one user generate queries at the same point of time on the same database. Concurrency makes it easy for the users to have access to the data at the same time, according to the policies defined by the organization or the database.

2.9. CONSIDERATIONS FOR SELECTION OF DATABASE

There are several factors that come into play to make a choice on the types of database and the products of relational database. The choice of the RDBMS completely depends on the needs of the business. However, the questions that may be answered for the selection may involve:

- **Requirement of Data Accuracy:** Is there a possibility of the storage of data and its accuracy to depend on the business logic and if there is a strict requirement for the data to be accurate such as in financial data and government reports.

- **Need for Scalability:** It is important to know the scale at which the data to be managed is and the growth that may be anticipated with that data. It is also important to know is the model for database needs to support the copies for database and in that case if it can maintain the consistency.
- **Concurrency:** The important question is also if there will be a situation in which there will be multiple users and applications who require simultaneous access and if the software support concurrency with simultaneous protection of data.
- **Performance and Reliability Needs:** It is important to know if there is the need of product that delivers high performance and reliability and what the requirements are for the performance on the response to the queries.

2.10. THE RELATIONAL DATABASE OF THE FUTURE: THE SELF-DRIVING DATABASE

Over the years, relational databases have gotten better, faster, stronger, and easier to work with. But they've also gotten more complex, and administering the database has long been a full-time job. Instead of using their expertise to focus on developing innovative applications that bring value to the business, developers have had to spend most of their time on the management activity needed to optimize database performance.

Today, autonomous technology is building upon the strengths of the RM to deliver a new type of relational database. The *self-driving database* (also known as the *autonomous database*) maintains the power and advantages of the RM but uses artificial intelligence (AI), machine learning, and automation to monitor and improve query performance and management tasks.

For example, to improve query performance, the self-driving database can hypothesize and test indexes to make queries faster, and then push the best ones into production—all on its own. The self-driving database makes these improvements continuously, without the need for human involvement.

Autonomous technology frees up developers from the mundane tasks of managing the database. For instance, they no longer have to determine infrastructure requirements in advance.

Instead, with a self-driving database, they can add storage and compute resources as needed to support database growth. With just a few steps, developers can easily create an autonomous relational database, accelerating the time for application development.

2.11. CONCLUSION

Relational databases are an integral part of the data storage systems. They help regulate and manipulate the data as per the convenience of the users and are ideal for tabulating and manipulating the data. There are several relational databases that are in operation today and most popular ones work on SQL.

The relational databases find their use and application in several verticals such as financial issues, reporting in government and global organizations, transactions from various platforms, record keeping and many more. They provide the advantages such as that of concurrency, consistency, atomicity, data integrity, accuracy, and durability.

They help keep the data secure and private, while providing multiple access for simultaneous entities. There is a wide range of ways in which the relational databases can be used in the future and improve the data handling systems for the various organization.

REFERENCES

1. Homan, J., (2014). *Relational vs Non-Relational Databases*. [online] Pluralsight.com. Available at: https://www.pluralsight.com/blog/software-development/relational-non-relational-databases (accessed on 1 June 2020).
2. Ibm.com. (2019). *Relational-Databases*. [online] Available at: https://www.ibm.com/cloud/learn/relational-databases (accessed on 1 June 2020).
3. Oracle.com. (n.d.). *What is a Relational Database?* [online] Available at: https://www.oracle.com/in/database/what-is-a-relational-database/ (accessed on 1 June 2020).
4. Sisense. (n.d.). *What is a Relational Database Management System? | Sisense Glossary*. [online] Available at: https://www.sisense.com/glossary/relational-database/ (accessed on 1 June 2020).
5. The Relational Data Model, (n.d.). [ebook] Available at: http://infolab.stanford.edu/~ullman/focs/ch08.pdf (accessed on 1 June 2020).

CHAPTER 3

Overview of Computer Networking

CONTENTS

3.1. Introduction 54

3.2. Computer Network 54

3.3. Computer Networking 56

3.4. Computer Network Components 61

3.5. Some Protocols For Computer Networking 68

3.6. Types of Network 69

3.7. Internetwork 77

3.8. Conclusion 81

References 82

Computer networks have helped connect the globalized world. It is an integral part of daily life in the modern world. This chapter explains the meaning of the computer network along with it uses advantages and disadvantages. It then covers important aspects of computer networking such as network design and topology. The chapter then describes hardware and software which are important components of computer networks. The next topic covered is protocols for computer networking. The chapter finally explains various types of networks, which are formed by the networking of various computer systems and networks.

3.1. INTRODUCTION

Computer networks are an integral part of modern life. A computer network is used for the simplest of things like the withdrawal of cash from an automated teller machine (ATM). Sending mails and browsing the internet also takes place through a computer network which is known as the internet.

There is a compelling presence of computer networks on human lives. Telemarketers also make use of networking to sell their products. People watch various channels on their television through computer networks. These transport programs onto the TV screens. The mobile phone which is an integral part of modern life is connected by networks, without which it will just be a battery powering-up a meaningless screen.

Computer networks provide these extraordinary services. They are responsible for the transfer of data to and from the televisions, cell phones, computers, and other modern machines. There are applications, which are a part of the network and translate these data. These get projected as TV images, icons on PC screens, and text messages.

The networks fetch data from all parts of the world. The tasks are performed by these networks in a second or even less irrespective of the distance.

3.2. COMPUTER NETWORK

A computer network comprises of two or more connected computers. There are two aspects of these connections:

- The physical connection is through wires, cables, and wireless media such as cell phone; and

- The logical connection is through the physical media through which data is transported.

The networking computers comprises of more than just physical connectors like ports on the PC and electrical plugs. The computer networking or exchange of data happens through several basic rules.

Figure 3.1: Representation of computer network.

Source: Image by Pixabay.

3.2.1. Uses of Computer Networks

Some common applications of computer networks are discussed below:

- Network allow the user to share resource such as files, printers;
- The participants can share expensive software's and database through network;
- Networks allows users to exchange data and information; and
- Facilitates fast and effective communication between the different computers in the network.

3.2.2. Advantages of a Computer Network

Some benefits of computer network are:

- Network allows to connect multiple computers together enables sharing information when accessing the network; and

- Electronic communication over computer network is cheaper and more.

3.2.3. Disadvantages of Computer Networks

The disadvantages of computer network are:

- The initial set-up cost of network is high as it involves investment in hardware and software;
- Appropriate security precautions are required such as firewalls, encryptions, etc. to protect the firewall as your data will be at considerable risk;
- Requires constant administration and hence involves time;
- Requires regular maintenance as server failure and cable faults may occur; and
- Some components of the network may have a short life and has to be repaired or replaced.

3.3. COMPUTER NETWORKING

Computer networking is the practice by which two or more computing devices are interfaced with each other. The main objective of networking is sharing of data among the users. Computer networks comprises of hardware as well as software.

There are several ways in which computer networks can be categorized. One approach for categorizing is according to the geographic area that it covers. Local area network (LAN) is limited to a small area such as a single school, home or a small office. WAN offers a wider coverage across spanning over several cities, states. The largest WAN is the internet which covers the world.

These different types of networks are discussed in detail in the following sections.

3.3.1. Network Design

Network design comprises of a category of system designs which is concerned with the data transport mechanism. Network design also has an analysis stage in which the requirements are generated. It occurs before the implementation stage in which the system or the relevant system component is constructed.

The main objective of network design is to satisfy the requirements if data communication and also minimize the expense of the same. The scope of the network design can vary from one network design project to another. It is determined by factors such as geographic peculiarities and the nature of the data that will be transported over the network.

There are several computer networks each of which has its own design. There are two basic forms of network designs namely client-server and peer-to-peer (P2P). Client-server networks comprises of centralized server computers. These store email, web pages, files, and applications. These are accessed by the computers of the client and other devices as well.

On the other hand, P2P network comprises of devices that support the same functions. Business use client-server networks which, P2P network is common in households.

3.3.2. Network Topology

Network topology is an arrangement of network which comprises of nodes and connecting lines via sender and receiver. It defines the network layout or structure from the perspective of data flow. For example, data flows occur through one centralized device, whereas in bus networks all computers share and communicate across a common conduit.

3.3.3. Home Computer Networking

Home computer networks belong to homeowners with minimal technical background, unlike other networks which are built and maintained by engineers. The broadband routers used in home networks ae simple and easy to set up. These networks are installed by household members to share files and printers in different rooms and provide access to files and printers to all members of the household. It also improves overall network security.

Advancement in technology has improved the capability of each generation. Earlier, people home networks were set up to connect a few PCs, share files and resources like printers. In the present day, networks also connect game consoles, digital video recorders, and smart phones for streaming sound and video. Home automation is another example of home network. Though it has existed for many years, these have become more popular in recent times with practical systems which can control digital thermostats, lights, and appliances.

3.3.4. Business Computer Networks

Small and home office make use of simple technology which is comparable with the home networks. However, the needs of business are more than the requirements of home networks. It needs additional data storage, communication, and security requirements which requires the expansion of networks in different ways. This is particularly important when the business expands.

The business network typically needs multiple LANs, while the home network on the other hand, only uses one LAN. Organizations which have buildings in multiple locations, make use of wide area networks (WANs) which facilitates the connection of branch offices together.

Voice over IP is also used in some of the households, but it is it more prevalent in businesses along with network storage and back up technologies. Intranets are used by larger companies to maintain the company websites, as well as help business communication among the employees (Figure 3.2).

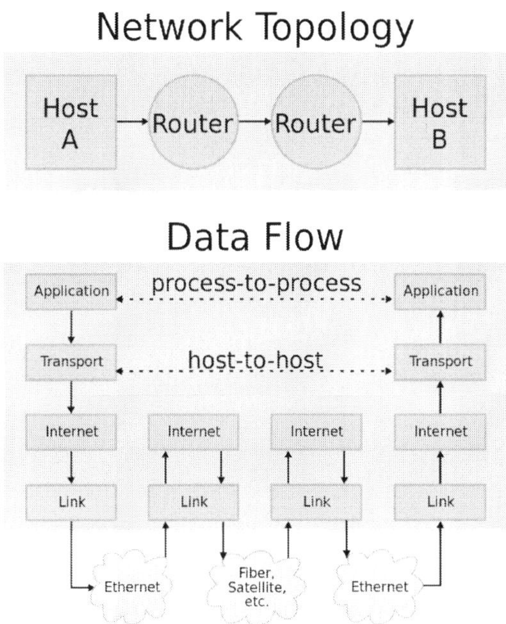

Figure 3.2: Representation of network topology.

Source: Image by Wikimedia Commons.

The star, bus, mesh, and ring are common types of topology.

- Mesh Topology

In this topology, the connection among the various devices is established through a particular channel. Dedicated channels are used to connect the devices to each other. These channels are known as links. Let us consider an example to understand mesh topology.

Suppose a mesh topology comprises of N number of devices, then each device would require N-1 number of ports. The total number of dedicated links that it would require is $^{N}C_{2}$, i.e., N (N-1)/2.

Therefore, if 5 devices are connected to each other, them the total number of ports required is 4. The total number of links required in this case is 5*4/2 = 10.

There are several advantages of mesh topology:

- Mesh technology is robust.
- Any fault in the network can be easily diagnosed.
- The data transmitted is reliable because data is transferred among devices using dedicated links or channels.
- The security and privacy of data is high.

There are some challenges associated with this topology:

- The installation and configuration of mesh topology is challenging.
- It has a high maintenance cost.
- The need for bulk wiring makes the cost of cables high. Therefore, it is suitable for less number of devices.
- Star Topology

Star topology, there is a single hub which connects all the devices. This single hub is the central node to which all other nodes are connected. The hubs can be either active or passive. The active hubs are intelligent and have repeaters attached to them. The passive hubs are not intelligent, for example broadcasting devices.

The main advantages of this technology are:

- There is clarity regarding the number of cables required to connect the devices. If there are N number of devices, there are N cables. So, it is easy to set up.
- There is only 1 port required to connect the device to the hub.

The challenges of star topology are:

- The whole system will crash down if the concentrator (hub) on which the topology relies fails.
- It has a high installation cost.
- A single concentrator, the hub determines the performance of this topology.
- Bus Topology

Bus topology is a network type in which a single cable connects every computer and the network device. The transmission of data from one end to another end in unidirectional. This topology does not support bi-directional transmission of data.

In many networks, the bus topology has a shared backbone cable. There are drop lines which connects the nodes to channels.

The advantages of this topology are as follows:

- If a topology has N devices connected to each other, then it requires 1 backbone cable and N drop lines to connect them.
- Compared to other topologies, the cost of cables in case of small networks.

The disadvantages of this topology are:

- The whole system will crash if the common cable fails.
- There is an increased possibility of collision in this network if the traffic is heavy. Various protocols are used in MAC layer known as Slotted Aloha, Pure Aloha, and CSMA/CD, etc.
- Ring Topology

This topology is named so because it forms a ring connecting a device with its exactly two neighboring devices. It comprises of 4 stations which connect with each other to form a ring.

The operations that take place in the ring topology are as follows:

- It has one station, which is known as monitor station and takes the responsibility of performing the operations;
- The station has to hold the token to transmit the data. Once the

transmission is complete, the token is released so that other stations can use it;

- The token will circulate in the ring when there is no transmission of data by the station; and
- The ring topology has two types of token releases, namely early and delay token releases. In the case of the former, the token is releases just after the transmission of data. In case of the latter, the token is released after the acknowledgement is received from the receiver.

The main advantage of this topology is that the possibility of collision is minimum in this type of topology. Moreover, it is cheaper to install and expand.

The main challenge is with troubleshooting. The entire topology is disturbed if there is any addition or removal of stations between the topology.

- Hybrid Topology

Hybrid topology is a combination of two or more topologies which are described above. This topology is scalable and can be expanded easily. Though the topology is reliable, it is also expensive.

3.4. COMPUTER NETWORK COMPONENTS

Computer networks are made of both physical parts as well as software which is needed for installing computer networks, whether it is for official purpose or for domestic use. The hardware components include server, peer, client, transmission medium and connecting devices. Operating systems and protocols are a part of software components.

There are special purpose communication devices such as network routers, network cables, access points which keep the network together. The network operating systems and other software applications are responsible for creating network traffic and facilitate the users to do useful things (Figure 3.3).

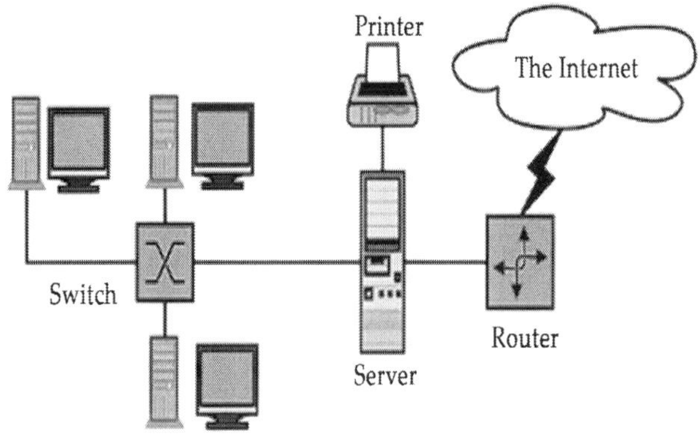

Figure 3.3: The various components of computer network.

Source: Image by Wikipedia.

3.4.1. Hardware Components

The network hardware comprises of a several devices which are explained below:

- **Servers:** These are high-configuration computers which enable the management of the resources of the network. The server generally has a network operating system which gives the user access to the network resources. There are different kinds of servers such as database servers, file servers, print servers, etc.
- **Clients:** These are computers that request and receive service from the servers to access and use the resources of the network.
- **Peers:** These are computers that provide and receive services from other peers in the workgroup network.
- **Transmission Media:** These are channels which facilitate the transfer of data from one device to another in a network. It may be guided or unguided media. Examples of former are fiber optic cables, coaxial cable, etc., examples of latter are microwaves, infra-red waves.
- **Connecting Devices:** These devices bind the network media together and act as middleware connecting the computers or networks. The commonly used connecting devices are:
- **Routers:** It is a hardware whose main function is to receive, analyze from a network and move incoming packets to another

network. The other functions of router include the conversion of packets to another network interface, drop them and perform other actions with respect to the network.

The router has highest capability among all connecting devices since it also analyses data besides transferring it between the computers or network devices. It can also change the manner in which data is packed and send it over a different network. For example, routers are used in home networks to share a single Internet connection between multiple computers.

- **Bridges:** These are connecting devices that are used between networks in the data link layer of OSI model. The functionality of bridges is higher than Layer 1 devices such as hubs and repeaters. They are used to segment networks which have grown to a point at which data traffic slows down the global transfer of information through the physical environment of the network.
- Hubs: It is a common connection point for devices in a network and is also referred to as network hub. It comprises of several ports and are used widely to connect segments of a LAN. When one port receives a packet, it is copied to other ports so that all segments of the LAN can access all the packets.

There are three types of hubs, passive hubs, intelligent hubs and switching hub. A passive hub acts as a conduit for the data which enables it to go from one device to another. These intelligent hubs have other features which helps the administrator to monitor the traffic which is passing through the hub. It also helps in configuring each port in the hub.

These are also referred to as manageable hubs. Another type of hub is the switching hub, which can identify the destination address of each packet and then forward it to the correct port.

- **Repeaters:** These are network devices which operates at a physical layer of OSI model. The main function is to amplify or regenerate an incoming signal and subsequently retransmit it. Hence, they are also called boosters.

The coverage area is expanded by incorporating repeaters in networks. When the transmission of an electrical signal occurs via a channel, it gets attenuated. The factor that determines this is the nature of the channel or the technology. A limitation is therefore imposed on the length of the LAN or coverage area of cellular networks. One way to mitigate this problem is to install repeaters at certain intervals.

The attenuated signal is amplified by the route and subsequently retransmitted. Often there is a loss of signal which takes place during data transmission which can be reconstructed using digital repeaters. Hence repeaters are widely incorporated to connect between two LANs. This enables the formation of a large single LAN.

Gateways: It is a key stopping point when data is being transmitted to or from other networks. Gateway enables the communication of data back and forth of the network. Without the gateway, the internet will not be useful. In case of business organizations, gateway is the system which is responsible for routing traffic from a workstation to the outside network that is serving up the Web pages.

In case of basic home internet connections, the gateway is the Internet Service Provider which provides the user with the access to the entire Internet. When the gateway is the computer, it also functions as a firewall and a proxy server. A firewall is responsible for preventing unwanted traffic and outsiders from accessing a private network.

A proxy server is one which is placed between programs on the computer like a Web browser and a computer server which the user uses. The function of the proxy server is to ensure that —the real server is able to handle the online data requests.

- **Switches:** It is a high-speed connecting device which receives the incoming data packets over a LAN and sends them to their destination. A LAN switch operates at the data link layer also referred to as Layer 2 or the network layer of the OSI Model. Therefore, it is capable of supporting all types of packet protocols. In other words, switches handle the traffic in a simple LAN. Though their functions are similar to hubs, they are much smarter.

The only function of a hub is to simply connect all the nodes on the network. The communication which is facilitated in this manner is haphazard. Any device can try to communicate at any time which increases the chances of collisions. A switch eliminates this challenge by creating an electronic tunnel for a fraction of a second, between source and destination ports.

This cannot be penetrated by any other traffic thereby facilitating communication without any collisions. The functions of switches are comparable to routers as well, however, a router also has the ability to forward packets between different networks. However, in case of a switch, the communication is limited to node-to-node when transmitting over the same network.

3.4.2. Software Components

The two most important software components are Network Operating Systems and Protocol Suite.

- **Networking Operating System:** It is installed in the server and its main function is to facilitate the sharing of files, database, applications, printers, etc. in a network. It is an operating system which manages the resources of the network. In other words, it is an operating system which includes special functions which enables the connection of computers and devices into a LAN.

The networking operating system is capable of managing several inputs or request parallely. It ensures the required security in a multiuser environment. The system can operate in two ways. It can either be completely self-contained operating system such as in case of as UNIX, NetWare, Windows 2000, or Mac OS X. Or it may depend in an existing operating system for proper functioning. For example, LAN Server requires OS/2; Windows 3.11 for Workgroups requires DOS.

There are other functions which an NOS may provide besides file and print services such as directory services, messaging system, multiprotocol routing capabilities and network management.

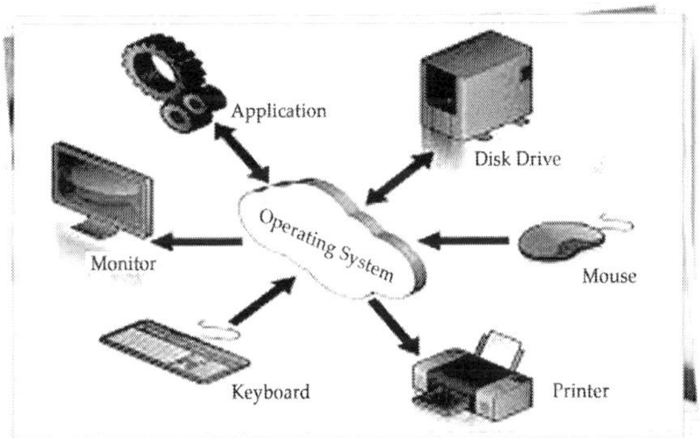

Figure 3.4: The network operating system provides multiple services.

Source: Image by Wikipedia.

- **Protocol Suite:** Protocol refers to rule or guideline which each computer follows for data communication. The protocol suit refers to a set of related protocols which computer networks should adhere to. Popular protocol suites are OSI Model (Open System Interconnections and TCP/IP Model.

It is a standard network model and communication protocol stack which is used widely, such as on the Internet and also other computer networks. There are other networking models, but the IP suite is the most widely used global standard which is used for computer-to-computer communication.

The client/server model is the basis for the IP suite. In this model several there are several client programs which share the services of a single server program. In this suite, the protocols define end-to-end data handling methods for a wide range of functions such as packetizing, addressing and routing to receiving.

The IPS is broken down to layers and comprises of the link layer, the internet layer, the transport layer, application layer and the physical layer.

The protocols for communication in each layer are specific. At times, the suite is referred to as TCP/IP since these protocols are used predominantly in this model and were the first protocol suite to be used. There are several other protocols in an IP suite.

Some of the protocols in each layer are explained below:

1. Application layer:
   - BGP
   - FTP
   - HTTP
   - NNTP
   - NTP
   - DHCP
   - DNS
   - POP
   - ONC/RPC
   - IMAP
   - LDAP
   - MGCP
   - RTP
   - RTSP
   - RIP
   - SIP

- SMTP
- SNMP
- SSH
- Telnet
- TLS/SSL
- XMPP.

2. Transport layer:
   - DCCP
   - RSVP
   - SCTP
   - TCP
   - UDP
3. Internet layer:
   - IP
   - IPv4
   - IPv6
   - ICMP
   - ICMPv6
   - ECN
   - IGMP
   - IPsec
4. Data link layer:
   - ARP
   - DSL
   - Ethernet
   - FDDI
   - ISDN
   - L2TP
   - MAC
   - NDP
   - OSPF
   - PPP

(Defense Advanced Research Projects Agency (DARPA) conducted research and developed the Internet protocol (IP) suite for the United States Department of Defense (DoD). Hence, the model is also referred to as the DoD model.

3.5. SOME PROTOCOLS FOR COMPUTER NETWORKING

The communication language which the computer devices use is called network protocols. Different networks have different protocols and each of it supports a specific application. The most widely used protocol is the TCP/IP which is found in the internet and home networks. The basic protocols which all networks follow is discussed below.

3.5.1. Same Procedures

All the machines in the network must send and receive data following the same procedures. These are referred to as communication protocols. The devices on a network may at times follow different protocols. Then protocol converters are used to convert these protocols. The function performed by a converter can be compared to a translator who translates two languages.

An example is a person can send email from wire-based computer which can be accessed from cell phone over internet. For the reader, conversions are performed at the physical level. The wire-based images are converted into wireless-based images. There is a conversion happening at the logical level from email format to the text format. The protocol converter is provided and the receiver or the sender is not required to deal with it.

3.5.2. Prevent Data Corruption

The data transmission should occur without corruption. If the message sent in Hello Mom, it must be received at the other end in the same form and not say Hello Tom. Therefore, a mechanism is required whereby the receiving computer acknowledges that uncorrupted data has been received and confirm with the sending computer if the data was received in error.

Therefore, if the receiver receives the message Hello Tom, she will not see this erroneous message on her screen. A software at the receiver's end will check the data and return a message to the sender computer requesting retransmission. These processes occur in a fraction of a second. Therefore, both the sender and the receiver are not aware of the short delay in the ongoing dialogue.

3.5.3. Determine Origin and Destination

The computers in the network should be able to determine where the data is originating from and its destination. If the receiver wants to send a response, the network should be able to route it back to the sender. The receiver's device must be able to provide the address to the network. The receiver and the sender must not be concerned with these tasks. The assignment of addresses happens automatically. This is a service that networking offers to network users.

In order for correct exchange of data between computers, standardized addresses are required. There are innumerable computers around the world which can be networked. The addresses of these computers must be scalable so that a large number of computers can be accommodated.

3.5.4. Prevent Hacking

Hacking is a security threat which must be prevented so that the hackers do not damage computers and files. Security and management of network is important and there should be a method for identifying and verifying the devices connected to a network.

Unethical hackers try to exploit weaker points in a network system in order to gain unauthorized access into the system and steal confidential information. There are some "black-hat hackers" who are driven by vicious motives to wreak havoc on security systems. Some may also do it for exchange for money.

The networks of some organizations in particular are at an increased risk of being hacked such as corporate houses, financial institutions and security establishment. Therefore, proper security management is important to secure networks from these threats.

The above mentioned is not an exhaustive list of network requirement. There are several issues that may occur when exchange and sharing of data takes place between two devices on a network. These rules help in minimizing these issues and risks and facilitate the transfer.

3.6. TYPES OF NETWORK

Networks are of various types. Some of them are as simple as a point-to-point connection between two computers in which files are transferred to each other. Others are complex, such as transfer of funds between accounts in a banking system.

Another type of complex network is cellular network. It tracks the person connected to it across terrains and hands over the connection to the next wireless tower to which the person has moved. These networks can be according to their size and purpose.

The size of network is expressed in terms of geographic area and the number of computers present in the network. It encompasses systems present in a single room to millions of devices spread across a wide area. The types of network which are found are

- PAN;
- LAN;
- MAN; and
- WAN.

3.6.1. Personal Area Network (PAN)

Personal area network or PAN is arranged around a person typically within the range of 10 meters. This network is a simple one which is used for personal purpose. It comprises of devices such as computer, mobile, media player, play stations or personal digit assistant. PAN is used to establish communication between these personal devices which enables them to connect to digital network and internet.

PAN was first developed from the due to the work of Thomas Zimmerman, a research scientist. It is equipped to cater to a small area and generally handles the interconnection of IT devices at the surrounding of a single user. Appliances such as keyboards, cordless mice, and Bluetooth systems are used by the user.

The advantage of PAN is that it is more safe and secure. This is because it only offers short range solutions of up to ten meters and so cannot be hacked from distant networks. This disadvantage is that it is not capable of establishing strong connection to other network at the same radio bands. Moreover, there are limitations with respect to distance as it is restricted to a small area.

The PAN cam be classified into two types:

- Wired Personal Area Network; and
- Wireless Personal Area Network.

Wireless PAN is based on wireless technologies such as Bluetooth, wireless fidelity (Wi-Fi), and others. It has a low range of connectivity. Wired PAN is created by using the Universal Serial Bus an industry standard which sets requirement for cables and connectors. It also establishes protocols for connection, communication, and power supply between computers, peripheral devices and other computers.

Some examples of examples of PAN are discussed below:

- **Body Area Network**: Body area network is one which moves along a person. A commonly used body area network is mobile network.
- **Offline Network**: An offline network is one which is created inside the home. Hence it is also referred to as home network. It is developed to integrate several devices such as computer, television, printers. However, internet connection is not present.
- **Small Home Office:** It enables the connection of a wide range of devices to the internet. It uses a VPN to connect these devices to a corporate network.

3.6.2. Local Area Network (LAN)

A Local Area Network or LAN comprises of a group of computer and peripheral devices which are used to establish network in a small area, such as school, home, laboratory, office, and home. It is useful for sharing resources like files, printers, and other applications. In most cases, LAN is used as an additional medium of transmission.

The interconnected devices in LAN is generally less than 5000 though it may spread across several buildings. It uses communication medium such as twisted pair, coaxial cable and others to connect these devices. The hardware used are hubs, Ethernet cables and network adapters which are not expensive. Data transmission occurs at an extremely fast rate over these networks. It also offers a high security level.

Some important characteristics of LAN are:

- It is not governed by any regulatory body as it is a private network;
- The speed of LAN is higher than other WAN systems; and
- Several access control methods are used such as token ring and Ethernet.

The advantages of using LAN are as follows:

- The same software can be used over the network and there is no need to purchase licensed software for every client which the network connects;

- The hardware used are digital versatile disc-read only memory (DVD-ROM) hard-disks, and printers to share the LAN. Hence the cost of hardware purchases is much lower;
- All the data can be managed at one place which makes it more secure;
- A single hard disk of the server computer is enough to store data of all network users;
- Data and messages can be transferred easily over the networked computers; and
- It enables the sharing of a single network connection among all the users of LAN.

There are disadvantages of LAN which are as follows:

- The privacy is not good, since LAN admin can check personal data files of every user connected to LAN;
- Though the use of shared computer resources in LAN will result in cost savings, the initial cost of installing LANs makes it expensive;
- There is a need for constant LAN administration. This is because LAN has issues related to software setup and hardware failures; and
- Unauthorized users can gain access sensitive data of an organization. In order to prevent this, it is important to secure centralized data repository.

3.6.3. Wide Area Network (WAN)

Wide Area Network (WAN) is another important computer network that which is spread across a large geographical area even across states or countries. This network is bigger than the LAN. It connects to a large geographical area through telephone line, satellite links and fiber optic cable.

WAN network system could be a connection of a LAN which connects with other LAN's using telephone lines and radio waves. It is mostly limited to an enterprise or an organization. The biggest WAN in the world is the internet. It is used widely in the field of Business, education, and government.

All users share the software files and have access to the latest files. Global integrated network can be built using WAN.

The biggest advantage of WAN is that it helps you cover a large geographical area. This facilitates communication among businesses which are situated at a distance. The WLAN connections use radio transmitters and receivers which are built into client devices. It also supports devices like laptop, mobile phones, computers, and tablet.

However, WAN also has certain drawbacks. It has a high initial set up cost. Moreover, WAN needs skilled technicians and network administrators to maintain it. It is a complex network and covers a large area and hence errors and issues could crop up.

The time to resolve issues is also more since several wired and wireless technologies are used. The security and safety over WAN are comparatively lowers than other types of network.

Some examples of Wide Area Network are:

- **Mobile Broadband:** A 4G network has an extensive usage and s spread over a large region or country
- **Last Mile Connectivity:** A telecom company can be used to provide last mile connectivity. It provides internet services to the customers spread across several cities by connecting their home with fiber.
- **Private Network:** Organizations can use WAN to connect different offices. This is enables by using a telephone leased line which a telecom company provides.
- There are several advantages of Wide Area Network which are explained below:
- **Geographical Area:** The area covered by WAN is large. It allows businesses to connect to its branches in different cities. This networking takes place through leased lines which connects one branch to another.
- **Centralized Data:** WAN offers centralized data to its users. Hence, there is no need for backing up of emails, files or back up servers.
- **Updated Files:** The users work on live servers, which means any changes made to the files are immediately updated. Programmers can access the updated files instantaneously.
- **Global Business:** Organizations can engage in business over the internet globally.
- **Sharing of Resources and Software:** WAN network enables

sharing of software and other resources such as RAM and hard drive.

- **Exchange Messages:** WAN network allows very fast transmission of message. It supports several applications such as WhatsApp, Facebook, and Skype which allows the users to communicate with friends and family.
- **High Bandwidth:** The use of leased lines for WAN networking gives high bandwidth. The high bandwidth increases the speed of transfer of data. This increases the productivity of the organization.

The following are the disadvantages of Wide Area Network:

- **Firewall and Antivirus Software:** WAN relies on internet for transfer of data. Therefore, it can be hacked and stolen by people with unscrupulous intentions. Virus can be injected into the system, making it necessary to use antivirus to protect the network.
- **Troubleshooting Problems:** Since WAN is extended over a large area, it is difficult to troubleshoot if any problem arises.
- **High Setup Cost:** WAN requires many supporting devices such as switches and routers and hence the cost of installing WAN network is high.
- **Security Issue:** WAN is a combination of all technologies which gives rise to security problems as compared to LAN and MAN.

3.6.4. Metropolitan Area Network (MAN)

A Metropolitan Area Network or MAN comprises of a computer network which is spread across an entire city, campus, college or a region. While LAN is limited to a single building of site, MAN covers a larger area than LAN. It extends over a large geographic area and is formed with the interconnection of different LAN which forms a larger network.

Telephone exchange lines, optical fibers and cables are used to connect various LANs. The MAN could have several configurations, each of which has a separate coverage area ranging from several miles to tens of miles. Hence the range of MAN is higher than LAN. However, the maximum range that it can cover is 50 km.

MAN is used widely by government agencies to connect the citizens and the private industries. There are several protocols used in MAN, the most important ones being RS-232, Frame Relay, ATM, ISDN, OC-3, ADSL, etc. It has high data rates which is sufficient for distributed computing applications.

MAN has its advantages as well as disadvantages. The advantages are:

- The communication is quite fast because it uses high-speed carriers such as fiber optic cables;
- It can include some parts of the city or the entire city;
- In case of extensive size network, it offers excellent support and greater access to WANs; and
- MAN has dual bus, which enables the transmission of data in both the directions concurrently.

The disadvantages of MAN are:

- It may be difficult to secure the system from hackers in case of MAN; and
- MAN requires more cable to establish connection between different places.

3.6.5. Other Types of Networks

The above mentioned are the broad types of networks. Apart from these there are other important types of networks:

- WLAN (Wireless Local Area Network);
- Storage Area Network;
- System Area Network;
- Home Area Network;
- POLAN-Passive Optical LAN;
- Enterprise private network;
- Campus Area Network; and
- Virtual Area Network.

These are discussed in detail below.

- **WLAN:** Wireless LAN is used to connect a single device or multiple devices using wireless communication. It is generally spread over a small area like home, school, or office building. The users can move around a local coverage area. This may be connected to the WLAN. In the present day, IEEE 802.11 standards guides the WLAN systems.

- **Storage-Area Network (SAN):** A Storage Area Network is a dedicated high-speed network or sub network which provides access to consolidated, block-level data storage. It forms an interconnection and presents shared pools of storage devices to multiple servers. It is commonly used to make storage devices, such as optical jukeboxes, disk arrays, and tape libraries.
- **System-Area Network:** System Area Network is a group of devices that are linked by a high-speed, high-performance connection over a local network. It is guided by the IP addresses, which are assigned by TCP/IP to each SAN network interface controller (NIC). This helps in determining data routing. The server-to-server and processor-to-processor applications is high-speed. All the computers connected act as a single system and operates at a high speed.
- **Passive Optical Local Area Network:** POLAN is a fiber-optic telecommunications technology for which enables the user to integrate into structured cabling. An advantage of this system is that it enables the resolution of the issues of supporting Ethernet protocols and network apps.

It makes use of optical splitter. This enables the user to separate an optical signal from a single-mode optical fiber. It enables the conversion of a single signal into multiple signals.

- **Home Area Network (HAN):** A HAN connects two or more computers creating a LAN in the confines of the home. This is useful when the homes have several computers used by different family members. For examples in US, almost 15 million have more than one computer. The network enables sharing of files, printers, programs, and other peripherals.
- **Enterprise Private Network:** Enterprise private network (EPN) are networks which business build and own. It enables the secure connection of numerous locations through which various computer resources can be shared. The businesses use it to interconnect various sites such as production sites, offices, and shops.

Companies which have disparate offices use thus type of network to establish a secure connection with those offices in order to share resources.

These private networks were first established in the early 1970s by AT&T. Telecommunications network were used to operate these networks. With the advancement in Internet technology the virtual private networks (VPNs) were developed. Encrypted data was transferred using public infrastructure.

The networks build by business organizations are still called EPNs security procedures and tunneling protocols are used to maintain the privacy of network. There are several advantages of EPN. They message transferred is secure because it is encrypted.

They are not as expensive and also scalable. They can maintain business continuity and help centralize IT resources.

- **Campus Area Network (CAN):** A Campus area network is made by connecting several interconnected LANs within a limited geographical area. For example, an educational institution can be linked to others through CAN to connect all the academic departments.

It is smaller than a MAN or WAN. It is also used extensively by corporates to link various departments and is referred to as corporate area network (CAN). There are several advantaged of CAN such as cost effectiveness. The network can also be built through wireless connections.

- **Virtual Private Network:** A VPN is a private network which connects remote sites or users together using a public network. It makes use of "virtual" connections which is routed to the remote site through the internet from the enterprise's private network or a third-party VPN service. The service can be paid or free for the user. It offers a secure means of web browsing over public Wi-Fi hotspots.

3.7. INTERNETWORK

An internetwork comprises of two or more computer network LANs or WAN or computer network segments. They are configured by a local addressing scheme and are connected using devices. The process of establishing these connections is known as internetworking.

Internetworking is basically the process by which intermediary devices such as routers or gateway devices. These have the ability to ensure error free data communication. These core devices are the backbone which enables internetworking. It ensures data communication among networks which various entities own and operate using a common data communication and the Internet Routing Protocol. It uses the Open System Interconnection (OSI) reference model.

The largest pool of networks is the internet which is located geographically throughout the world. The protocol stack TCP/IP is used to interconnect these networks. It is important for all connected network to use the same protocol stack or communication methodologies.

There are several underlying hardware technologies on which the internet is based. The IPs define a unified global address format. It also sets down the rules for formatting and handling packets. The participating networks are interconnected through routers.

The smallest internetwork is connection of two LANs of computers which are connected to each other through a router. There is a difference between internetworking and expanding the original LAN. When two LANs are connected using a switch or a hub it is an expansion of the original LAN and does not imply networking.

3.7.1. Interconnection of Networks

Internetworking was initially developed to establish a connection between two disparate types of networking technology. It became popular because of the increasing need develop a WAN to connect two or more LAN. Initially, the term catenet was used to refer to these types of network.

Advanced Research Projects Agency Network (ARPANET) and the national physical laboratory (NPL) network were the first two interconnected networks. The network elements which were used in the ARPANET to connect individual networks was referred to as gateways. However, this term is not used frequently now because of the ambiguity with respect to functionally different devices.

The term router is used to refer to interconnecting gateways. The term internetwork encompasses the connection of other types of computer networks such as PAN. The following are the requirements of building an internetwork:

- A standardized scheme which will facilitate in addressing packets to any host on any participating network.
- Components are required to interconnect the participating networks by routing packets to their destinations. These are based on standardized addresses.
- A standardized protocol is required which defines format and the manner of handling transmitted packets.

There is another type of interconnection of networks which often occurs within enterprises at the Link Layer of the networking model. In other words, it takes place at the hardware-centric layer below the level of the TCP/IP logical interfaces. Network bridges and network switches are used to accomplish these interconnections which are termed incorrectly as internetworking.

However, the result is just a larger single sub network which does not employ internetworking protocols to traverse these devices. A single computer network can be divided into segments to convert into an internetwork. Routers can be used to logically divide the segment traffic.

The IP is used, but it does not provide a reliable packet service across the network. The architecture does not require intermediate network elements to maintain any state of the network. This function is assigned to the endpoints of each communication session.

An appropriate Transport Layer must be used to transfer data reliably. One such protocol is Transmission Control Protocol (TCP) which can offer a reliable stream. Some applications can work on simple and connection-less transport protocol. These are called User Datagram Protocol (UDP) in order to perform tasks which do not require reliable delivery of data. It is also helpful in case of applications such as video streaming which require real-time service.

3.7.2. Types of Internetwork

For a long time, organizations made use of in-house networks for networking among their computer in order to provide their staff with applications. These networks were expensive and often challenging to use. As internet became popular, its networking software was available widely and generally free of charge. Therefore, organizations began to use the same software for internal use.

There are broadly two types of internetwork, extranet, and intranet.

1. **Extranet:** An extranet is a network which is used for information sharing outside the company. It may also be shared by one or more organization. It works on IP, for example TCP. It is the lowest level of internetworking.

The access to extranet can be provided who belong to different companies. For example, the supplier of an organization may be provided access to the extranet in order to manage online ordering, order tracking and management of inventory. This eliminates the requirement of sending information to suppliers as they are allowed to self-service basis.

Hospitals may also provide access of their booking system to General practices so that they can make appointments for their patients.

It is important that extranets maintain high levels of efficiency. This because everyone should be able to access the same data in the same format. The communications over extranet can be encrypted over a VPN. Therefore, it is more secure than sending data over public internet.

The authorized users are provided log in credentials through which they can access the extranet. WAN, MAN, and other such computer networks are examples of extranet. Extranet cannot be comprised of a single LAN. It must have at least one connection to external network.

2 **Intranet:** It is a private network which is based on the IP such as TCP and IP. It is used exclusively by a company or business organization. It uses internet technology but is insulated from the global internet.

The intranet can be accessed only by the members of the organization or employees of the company. It is operated to share information and resources among the employees. It enables the conduct of business in groups of teleconferences.

There are various types of information which an organization would want to share, such as the upcoming events, various policies, newsletters. It also shares popular applications which the employees may require such as forms for holiday requests or to reclaim expenses. Employees need not rely on paperwork which speeds up the workflow.

The organization can improve the efficiency of intranet by adding more features to it. It acts like a portal which provides access to all the things that the users require for work. Firewalls are present which protects the intranet from the global internet.

The users who are outsiders can be given access over a VPN. The data transfer between the user's personal computer (PC) and intranet is encrypted.

There are several advantages of intranet:

- **Communication:** It is a simple network which facilitates inexpensive communication. It supports email, chat, etc. through which an employee can communicate with another.
- **Collaboration:** This is the most important feature. Several users can share information over this network; however, the information can only be accessed by authorized user.

- **Time-Saving:** Intranet saves time as it enables the sharing of information real time.
- **Cost Effective:** Intranet saves cost of taking multiple print outs. The users can see data and documents over the browser and share duplicate copies.

There are several disadvantages of intranet and extranet. In case of in-house network, the developers expect the applications to last for several years. Practically this may not be possible because websites can change every few months, similar too web standards and fashions. In other words, the organization may still be using obsolete browser such as Internet Explorer 6. The internal applications that they may have developed may not have been tested or adapted for more modern browsers.

3.8. CONCLUSION

A computer network is built by connecting two or more computers. They help in various functions such as sharing of resources, expensive database and software among participants. All exchange of information happens via network. Computer networks not only have a significance in the businesses, but also day-to-day activities such as withdrawal of money from ATM.

Networks can be categorized into many types based on the geographic area it covers and functions. A network topology is an arrangement of network which defines the network layout or structure from the perspective of data flow.

There are several components in a computer system which are categorized as hardware and software. Hardware represents the tangible portion while software is the intangible component which facilitates the functioning of the networks. There are several protocols which computer devices have to follow.

The major types of computer network are PAN, LAN, WAN and MAN, besides others such as virtual area network, system area network and others.

REFERENCES

1. Beal, V., (n.d.). *What is a Network Hub?* Webopedia Definition. [online] Webopedia.com. Available at: https://www.webopedia.com/TERM/H/hub.html (accessed on 1 June 2020).
2. Black, U., (2009). *An Overview of Networking | What Is a Network?* What Is Networking? | InformIT. [online] Informit.com. Available at: https://www.informit.com/articles/article.aspx?p=1353367 (accessed on 1 June 2020).
3. Computerhope.com. (2019). *What is a Router?* [online] Available at: https://www.computerhope.com/jargon/r/router.htm (accessed on 1 June 2020).
4. Guru99.com. (n.d.). *Types of Computer Networks: LAN, MAN, WAN, VPN.* [online] Available at: https://www.guru99.com/types-of-computer-network.html (accessed on 1 June 2020).
5. Mitchell, B., (2019). *Everything You Need to Know About Computer Networking From the Start.* [online] Lifewire. Available at: https://www.lifewire.com/what-is-computer-networking-816249 (accessed on 1 June 2020).
6. Schofield, J., (2010). *BBC-Web Wise-What are Intranets and Extranets*? [online] Bbc.co.uk. Available at: http://www.bbc.co.uk/webwise/guides/intranets-and-extranets (accessed on 1 June 2020).
7. Techopedia.com. (2011). *What is Enterprise Private Network?-Definition from Techopedia.* [online] Available at: https://www.techopedia.com/definition/26044/enterprise-private-network (accessed on 1 June 2020).
8. Techopedia.com. (2019). What is a Switch? - Definition from Techopedia. [online] Available at: https://www.techopedia.com/definition/2306/switch-networking (accessed on 1 June 2020).
9. Thakur, D., (n.d.). *Bridges-What is Bridges? Bridge Protocols.* [online] Ecomputernotes.com. Available at: http://ecomputernotes.com/computernetworkingnotes/communication-networks/bridges (accessed on 1 June 2020).
10. Tutorialspoint.com. (n.d.). *Computer Network Components.* [online] Available at: https://www.tutorialspoint.com/Computer-Network-Components (accessed on 1 June 2020).

11. Tutorialspoint.com. (n.d.). *What are Repeaters in Computer Network?* [online] Available at: https://www.tutorialspoint.com/what-are-repeaters-in-computer-network (accessed on 1 June 2020).
12. WhatIs.com. (n.d.). *What is Internet Protocol suite (IP suite)?- Definition from Whatis.com.* [online] Available at: https://whatis.techtarget.com/definition/Internet-Protocol-suite-IP-suite (accessed on 1 June 2020).
13. WhatIsMyIPAddress.com. (n.d*.). What is a Gateway?* [online] Available at: https://whatismyipaddress.com/gateway (accessed on 1 June 2020).
14. wikiHow. (2019). How to Stop Hackers from Invading Your Network. [online] Available at: https://www.wikihow.com/Stop-Hackers-from-Invading-Your-Network (accessed on 1 June 2020).
15. www.javatpoint.com. (n.d.). *Types of Computer Network-Javatpoint.* [online] Available at: https://www.javatpoint.com/types-of-computer-network (accessed on 1 June 2020).

CHAPTER 4

Principles of Distributed Database Systems

CONTENTS

4.1. Introduction 86

4.2. Distributed Database Design 89

4.3. Database Integration 95

4.4. Data Security 99

4.5. Types Of Transactions 103

4.6. Workflows 104

4.7. Integrity Constraints In Distributed Databases 105

4.8. Distributed Query Processing 106

4.9. Conclusion 109

References 111

For database management, it is very important to have a thorough understanding of the principles of the distributed database systems. This chapter discusses the principles of distributed database systems in detail. After introducing the concept of principles of distributed database systems, this chapter explains the process of database integration.

In this process, the entire process of schema mapping is explained. Also, this chapter discusses, the entire concept of data security along with explaining the importance of data security in database systems. There are various types of transactions models are used in the database management. These different transactions models are also discussed in this chapter.

Moreover, the nested transaction model is discussed in detail along with explaining the workflows. Later in this chapter, various integrity constraints in the distributed database systems are discussed. Lastly, this chapter talks about various processes in distributed query processing.

4.1. INTRODUCTION

Data independence is the fundamental principle behind data management. This allows applications and all the users to share data at a high conceptual level at the same time ignoring all the implementation details. This fundamental principle has been attained by database systems which provide advanced capabilities like high-level query languages, access control, transactions, automatic query processing and optimization, schema management, data structures for supporting complex objects, etc.

A distributed database is defined as a collection of multiple, logically interrelated databases that are distributed over the network of computer. A distributed database system is described as the software system that allows the management of the distributed database and helps in making the distribution transparent to all the users.

Distribution transparency helps in extending the principle of data independence. Extension of the principle of data independence by distribution transparency makes the invisible to the users. All these definitions believe that each site logically comprise a single, independent computer. Thus, each site is having the capability to execute all the applications on its own.

The sites are interconnected by the network of the computer. There is a loose connection between sites which function independently. Then, the applications can issue queries as well as transactions to the distributed database system. This transforms them into local queries and local transactions and integrates the final outcomes. It has to be noted that the distributed database system can run at any site s, not necessarily distinct from the data (that means it can be site 1 or site 2).

The database is distributed physically across the data sites. This is distributed by fragmenting and replicating the data. Provided a relational database schema, for example, fragmentation subdivides every single relation into partitions that is based on some function applied to some tuples' attributes. Each of the fragments may also be replicated in order to improve locality of reference (and hence performance) and availability. This is based on the user access patterns.

It has been observed that the use of a set-oriented data model (such as relational) has been vital to describe fragmentation. This is based on data subsets. The functions that are provided by a distributed database system could be the functions of a database system (access control, schema management, transaction support, query processing, etc.).

As these functions have to deal with distribution, they are more complicated to implement. Thus, there are many systems that support just a subset of these functions. When there is the already the existence of data and the databases, one is faced with the issue of providing integrated access to heterogeneous data. This process is called data integration.

Data integration consists in describing a global schema over the current data and mappings between the local database schema and the global database schemas. It has been observed that data integration systems have received various names. These names include multi-database systems, federated database systems, and, more recently, it has also been named as mediator systems.

Standard protocols like Java Database Connectivity (JDBC) and Open Database Connectivity (ODBC) ease data integration by the use of SQL. In the context of the Web, mediator systems help in allowing general access to autonomous data sources (like databases, files, documents, etc.) in read only mode. Therefore, they generally do not provide support to all the database functions like transactions and replication.

One can achieve a parallel database system by relaxing or not considering the architectural assumption of every single site as a logically single and independent computer system. This means a database system is implemented on a multiprocessor that is tightly-coupled or a cluster.

The presence of a single operating system is the main difference with a distributed database system. This operating system eases the process of implementation and also, the network is generally faster, and it is more reliable.

High-performance and high availability is the main objective of parallel database systems. High-performance (that is enhancing the transaction throughput or query response time) is achieved by exploiting data partitioning and query parallelism. On the other hand, high-availability is achieved by exploiting replication.

This has been made possible again by the use of a set-oriented data model. This helps in simplifying parallelism, mainly, independent parallelism that is between data subsets. It has to be noted that the distributed database approach has proved to be effective for those kinds of applications that can benefit from centralized control, static administration, and full-fledge database capabilities, for example, information systems.

The distributed database system generally runs on a separate server because of administrative reasons. This helps in reducing the scalability to tens of databases. It has been observed that Data integration systems obtain better scalability to hundreds or thousands of data sources by limiting the functionality (that is read-only querying).

In addition to it, the parallel database systems can also scale up to large configurations along with thousands of processing nodes. Although, both of these systems that is data integration systems and parallel database systems usually depends on a global schema. This global schema can be either centralized or replicated.

All the possible ways will be considered in which a distributed DBMS may be architected. There is the use of a classification that classifies the systems as characterized with respect to three dimensions. These dimensions are:

- the autonomy of local systems;
- their distribution; and
- Their heterogeneity.

In the context, autonomy, indicates to the distribution of control. It does not refer to the distribution of data. It refers to the extent to which individual DBMSs can function independently. The main aspect of autonomy is the distribution (or the decentralization) of control. On the other hand, the distribution dimension of the taxonomy focuses and handle the physical distribution of data over multiple sites (or nodes in a parallel system).

DBMSs have been distributed in a various number of ways. There is a difference between client/server (C/S) distribution and peer-to-peer (P2P) distribution (or it can be called full distribution). With client/server (C/S) DBMS, sites may be servers or clients, but they have different functionality. On the other hand, with homogeneous P2P DBMS, same functionality is provided by all the sites.

It should be noted that distributed database management system (DDBMS) came before client/server (C/S) DBMS in the late 1970. On the other hand, P2P data management struck back in the year of 2000 with "modern" variations to handle with very large scale, autonomy, and decentralized control.

Heterogeneity indicates to query languages, data models and transaction management protocols. In addition to autonomy and distribution, multi-database systems (MDBMS) deal with heterogeneity.

4.2. DISTRIBUTED DATABASE DESIGN

The design of a distributed computer system is basically concerned with taking the decisions or managing the placement of data and programs across various sites of a computer network, as well as possibly designing the network itself. As far as distributed data base management system is concerned, the distribution of applications mainly comprises two elements: the distribution of the distributed data base management system software and the distribution of the application programs that run on it.

Different architectural models play very pivotal role in addressing the issue of application distribution. In this chapter, distribution of data is discussed. It is important to note that the association of distributed systems can be investigated along three orthogonal dimensions which are discussed as follows (Levin and Morgan, 1975):

- Level of sharing;
- Behavior of access patterns; and
- Level of knowledge on access pattern behavior.

For level of sharing, there are three potentials. First, there is no sharing: this means that each application and its data execute at one site, and there is absence of communication with any other program or getting access to any data file located at other sites. This is very common at the time when networking started, but now a days it is not much in use.

We then find the level of data sharing; all the programs are replicated at all the sites, but it is not applicable in case of data files. Consequently, the requests of users are solved at the point of their generation and the needed data files are shifted around the network.

Finally, in data-plus-program sharing, it is possible to share both the both data and programs, which means that a program at a given site can demand for a service from another program located at a second site, which, in turn, can get access to a data file which is placed at a third site.

Levin and Morgan draw a distinction between data-plus-program sharing and data sharing to portray the differences between heterogeneous and homogeneous distributed computer systems. They try to explain the fact that in a heterogeneous environment, it is generally extremely difficult, and sometimes even impossible, to execute a given program on diverse hardware under a distinctive operating system. It might, be possible however, to transfer data around comparatively in an easy way.

Along the second dimension of access pattern behavior, it is generally feasible to find two substitutes. The access patterns of client requests may be inert, thus making it impossible to change over a time, or dynamic. It is usually comparatively easier to plan for and manage the inert environments than would most likely be the scenario dynamic distributed systems. Unfortunately, it is a challenging task to find many real-life distributed applications that would be conceived as inert. One question that is relevant to ask in this is not whether a system is dynamic or static, but how dynamic it is. Incidentally, it is along this dimension that the relationship between the query processing and distributed database design is established.

The third dimension of classification is the amount of knowledge or possession of information about the behavior of access pattern behavior. One likelihood in this, of course, is that the creators do not have embrace with any information or data about how users will access the database.

This is a theoretical possibility, but it is extremely difficult, in case not impossible, to create a distributed data base management system that can effectually address this situation. The more realistic substitutions are that the designers have comprehensive information, where the access patterns can practically be ascertained and do not diverge drastically from these predictions, or partial information, where there is higher possibility of diversion from the predictions.

4.2.1. Fragmentation

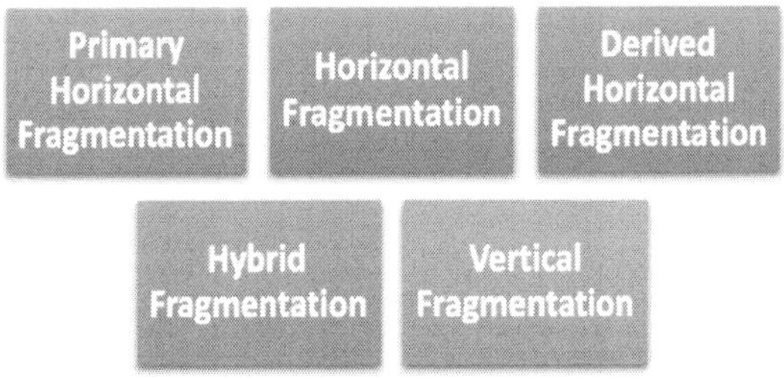

Figure 4.1: Different types of fragmentation.

In this section, the major area of focus in on the different types of fragmentation strategies and algorithms. As it is discussed previously, there are two primary fragmentation strategies: horizontal and vertical. In addition, there is also likelihood of nesting fragments in a hybrid fashion (Figure 4.1).

4.2.1.1. Horizontal Fragmentation

As it is discussed earlier, horizontal fragmentation partitions a relation along its tuples. Thus, it means each fragment has a subset of the tuples of the relation. There are basically two forms of horizontal partitioning: which is derived and primary. Primary horizontal fragmentation of a relation is usually done with the help of predicates that are defined on that relation.

While on the other hand, derived horizontal fragmentation, is the segregating of a relation that is the outcome from predicates being defined on another relation. In this section later, an algorithm is taken into consideration for executing both of these fragmentations. However, firstly, it is essential to investigate the needed information in a way to carry out horizontal fragmentation activity.

4.2.1.2. Information Requirements of Horizontal Fragmentation Database Information

The database information is majorly concerned with global conceptual schema. In this setting, it is worthy to note that how the relations between database are connected to one another, particularly with joins. In the relational model (RM), these relationships are also portrayed as relations. Although, in other data models, for instance in the entity-relationship (E-R) model (Chen, 1976), the relationships between database objects are explicitly illustrated. Ceri et al. (1983) also portrayed the relationship clearly, within the relational settings, for purposes of the distribution design.

In the latter notation, directed links are established between relations that are similar with each other by an equijoin operation. It is important to note that the direction of the link depicts a one-to-many relationship. For instance, for each title, there are number of employees with that title; thus, there is a clear relationship exists between the EMP a PAY relation. Along the same lines, the many-to-many relationship between the PROJ and EMP relations is articulated with two links to the ASG relation.

The links between database objects (i.e., relations in this scenario) should be relatively accustomed to those who have encountered with network models of data. In the RM, they are presented as join graphs, that will be discuss in detail later. It is introduced here because of the fact that they help to make it easier the presentation of the distribution models. The relation at the tail of a link is known by the name owner of the link and the relation at the head is known by the name the member (Ceri et al., 1983).

More frequently used terms, within the relational framework, are source relation in case of owner and target relation in case of member. Let us define two functions: owner and member, both of which play very important role in providing mappings from the set of links to the set of relations. Therefore, given a link, they return the owner or the member relations of the link, respectively

4.2.1.3. Primary Horizontal Fragmentation

Before giving the introduction about the formal algorithm for horizontal fragmentation, it is important to intuitively discourse the process for primary (and derived) horizontal fragmentation. A primary horizontal fragmentation can be defined as a selection operation on the owner relations of a database schema.

Therefore, for the given relation R, its horizontal fragments can be written as $Ri = \sigma Fi\ (R)$, $1 \leq i \leq w$ where Fi is the selection formula used to attain fragment Ri (also called the fragmentation predicate). It is important to note that if Fi is in conjunctive normal form, then it is a minterm predicate (mi). The algorithm that will be discussed, in fact, insist that Fi be a minterm predicate.

Now one can define the horizontal fragment in a more carefully and comprehensive way. A horizontal fragment Ri of relation R comprises of all the tuples of R that satisfy a minterm predicate mi. Hence, given a set of minterm predicates M, both the horizontal fragments of relation R and the minterm predicates are almost equivalent in number. This set of horizontal fragments is also frequently denoted as the set of minterm fragments.

From the prior discussion, it is right to say that the definition of the horizontal fragments relies on minterm predicates. Therefore, the first and foremost step for any fragmentation algorithm is to ascertain a pair of simple predicates that will create the minterm predicates. One essential facet of simple predicates is their completeness; other one is their minimalism.

4.2.1.4. Derived Horizontal Fragmentation

A derived horizontal fragmentation can be defined by a member relation of a link in accordance with a selection operation specified on its owner. It is utmost importance to keep two key points in mind. First, the exist relationship between the owner and the member relations can be defined as an equi-join. Second, an equi-join can be executed with the help of semi joins.

This second point is primarily essential for our personal objective, since there is need to have partition of a member relation in accordance with the fragmentation of its owner, but it also requires the resulting fragment to be defined only on the attributes of the member relation. Accordingly, given a link L where owner (L) = S and member (L) = R, the resulting horizontal fragments of R can be defined as Ri = RnSi, $1 \leq i \leq w$ where w refers to the highest number of fragments that will be defined on R, and Si = σFi (S), where Fi refers to the formula based upon which the primary horizontal fragment Si can be defined.

4.2.1.5. Vertical Fragmentation

It is important to keep in mind that a vertical fragmentation of a relation R yields fragments R1, R2, Rr, each of which contains a subset of R's attributes as well as the primary key of R. The major goal of vertical fragmentation is to divide a relation into a set of smaller relations in order to make sure that the majority of user applications will run on only one fragment. In this context, an "optimal" fragmentation refers to one that creates a fragmentation scheme which lessens the implementation time of user applications that run on these fragments.

Vertical fragmentation has been assessed in reference with the context of centralized database systems as well as distributed ones. Its motivation within the centralized context is as a design tool, which make it possible for the user queries to deal with smaller relations, resulting in allowing a smaller number of page accesses (Navathe et al., 1984). It has also been proposed that the most "active" sub relations can be recognized and positioned in a quicker memory subsystem in those cases where memory hierarchies are supported (Severance and Eisner 1976).

There are basically two types of heuristic approaches that are in existence for the vertical fragmentation of global relations:

- Grouping: it often starts by allotting each attribute to one fragment, and at each step, consistently joining some of the fragments until some criteria is accomplished. Grouping was first proposed for centralized databases (Hammer and Niamir, 1979), and was later used for distributed databases (Sacca and Wiederhold, 1985).
- Splitting: it basically starts with a relation and decides on beneficial partitioning rely on the access behavior of applications to the attributes. The technique was first recognized and used for centralized database design (Hoffer and Severance, 1975). Then, it was stretched to the distributed environment (Navathe et al., 1984).

4.2.1.6. Hybrid Fragmentation

In majority of the scenario, a simple vertical or horizontal fragmentation of a database schema will not be adequate enough to fulfill the requirements of user applications. In this scenario, a vertical fragmentation may be followed by a horizontal one, or vice versa, thus creating a tree structured partitioning. Since the two types of partitioning strategies can be used one after the other, this substitute is called hybrid fragmentation. It has also been known by the name nested fragmentation or mixed fragmentation.

One of the perfect examples of this is the requirement of hybrid fragmentation is relation PROJ, which has been is the consistent working in this area. Currently what is in existence is a horizontal fragment, each of which is further categorized into two vertical fragments.

It could be possible of higher number of levels of nesting, but it is surely finite. As far as horizontal fragmentation is concerned, one has to halt when each fragment comprises of only one tuple, whereas the termination point for that vertical fragmentation is one attribute per fragment.

However, these restrictions are quite academic, primarily because of the fact that the levels of nesting in most practical applications do not exceed. The key reason for this is that normalized global relations already have small degrees and it not viable to perform such large number of vertical fragmentations before there is sharp increase in the cost of joins.

4.2.2. Allocation

The distribution of resources across the nodes of a computer network is a long existing problem that has been studied broadly. It is generally seen that majority of work, however, does not able to solve the problem of distributed database design, but rather that of inserting individual files on a computer network. The key differences between the two will be examined shortly. First of all, the foremost important thing is to define the allocation problem more precisely.

4.3. DATABASE INTEGRATION

It has to be noted that database integration can be either physical or it can be logical (Jhingran et al., 2002). In the former, the source databases are integrated, and the integrated database is materialized. These are called data warehouses (DW).

Extract-transform load (ETL) tools is used for the integration. This tool allows the extraction of data from sources, the transformation of the data to match the GCS, and their loading (that is materialization). Enterprise Application Integration (EAI) enables the exchange of data between applications. In addition to it, it also performs same transformation functions, even though data are not completely materialized.

It has been observed that the global conceptual (or mediated) schema is completely virtual and not materialized in logical integration. This is also called Enterprise Information Integration (EII).

Both of these approaches are complementary, and these approaches also address different kind of needs. Data warehousing (Inmon, 1992; Jarke et al., 2003) aids decision support applications. These are commonly termed On-line Analytical Processing (OLAP) (Codd, 1995).

On-Line Transaction Processing (OLTP) applications like banking systems or airline reservation, are high-throughput transaction-oriented. There is the need of extensive data control and availability, fast response times and high multiuser throughput and predictable.

On the other hand, On-line Analytical Processing (OLAP) applications, like trend analysis or forecasting are required to evaluate historical, summarized data that is collected from a number of operational databases.

These applications make use of complicated queries over potentially large tables. It has to be noted that response time is important because of their strategic nature. Managers or analysts are the users. Performing On-line Analytical Processing (OLAP) queries directly over distributed operational databases give rise to two issues.

The first problem is that it hurts the performance of OLYP applications by competing for the required local resources. The second issue is that the overall response time of the On-line Analytical Processing (OLAP) queries can be very poor. The reason behind this poor response time is that the large quantities of data must be transferred over the network.

In addition to it, most On-line Analytical Processing (OLAP) applications do not require the latest versions of the data, and therefore, these applications do not require the direct access to most up-to-date operational data.

Therefore, DWs collect data from several operational databases and materialize them. All the updates that takes place on the operational database are propagated to the DW (it is also referred to as materialized view maintenance (Gupta and Mumick, 1999b)).

4.3.1. Bottom-Up Design Methodology

Bottom-up design includes the process by which the information that is collected from participating databases can be (physically or logically) integrated to form a single cohesive multi-database. In addition to it, there are two alternative approaches. It has been observed that in some of the cases, the global conceptual (or mediated) schema is defined in the beginning, in which case the bottom-up design includes mapping LCSs to this schema.

In DWs, this is the case. But the practice is not limited to these and there are some other data integration methodologies that may follow the same strategy. On the other hand, in other cases, the GCS is defined as an integration of parts of the local conceptual schemas (LCSs). The bottom-up design includes both the generation of the GCS as well as the mapping of individual LCSs to this GCS in this case.

The relationship between the GCS and the LCS can be of two fundamental types (Lenzerini, 2002), if the GCS is defined up-front. These two fundamental types are local-as-view (LAV), and global-as-view (GAV). The GCS definition exists in LAV systems, and each LCS is treated as a view definition over it.

On the other hand, the GCS is defined as a set of views over the LCSs in GAV systems. These views show that how the elements of the GCS can be derived, when it is required, from the elements of LCS.

One of the ways to think of the difference that is in between the two views is in terms of the results that can be attained from each system (Koch, 2001). In GAV systems, the query results are limited to the set of objects that are defined in the GCS, however the local DBMSs may be significantly richer.

On the other hand, in LAV systems, the results are constrained by the objects in the local DBMSs. In this case, the GCS definition may be richer. Therefore, in LAV systems, it may be required to deal with all the answers that are not complete.

It has been observed that the combination of these two approaches has also been proposed as global-local-as-view (GLAV) (Friedman et al., 1999). In this, the relationship between GCS and LCSs is specified by the use of both LAV systems and GAV systems.

Bottom-up design takes place in two general steps. These two steps consist of schema translation (or simply translation) and schema generation. In scheme translation, the first step, the component. Database schemas are translated to a common intermediate canonical representation (InS1, InS2., InSn). The use of a canonical representation helps in facilitating the translation process by decreasing the number of translators that are required to be written.

It has to be noted that the choice of the canonical model is vital. As a principle, it should be one that is suitably expressive to incorporate the concepts that are available in all the databases that will be integrated later on.

There are several other alternatives that have been used. These alternatives include the object-oriented model (Castano and Antonellis,

1999; Bergamaschi et al., 2001), entity-relationship model (Palopoli et al., 1998, 2003b; He and Ling, 2006), or a graph (Palopoli et al., 1999; Milo and Zohar, 1998; Melnik et al., 2002; Do and Rahm, 2002). All these alternatives may be simplified to a tree (Madhavan et al., 2001).

It has been observed that the graph (tree) models have become more popular as XML data sources have proliferated. In addition to it, it is fairly straightforward to map XML to graphs, but efforts are used to target XML directly (Yang et al., 2003).

4.3.2. Schema Mapping

It is required to identify how the data from each of the local databases (source) can be mapped to GCS (target) once a GCS (or mediated schema) is defined. It is also important to preserve the semantic consistency (as it is defined by both the source as well as the target).

However, schema matching has recognized the correspondences between the LCSs and the GCS, it might not have identified explicitly how to get all the global database from the local ones. This is what schema mapping is all about.

Schema mappings are used in order to explicitly get the data from the sources and translate the data to the DW schema for populating it. This is the case of warehouses. On the other hand, in the case of data integration systems, these schema mappings are used in query processing phase by both the query processor as well as the wrappers.

There are two issues that are related to schema mapping. These issues are mapping creation, and mapping maintenance. Mapping creation is defined as the process of making explicit queries that help in mapping the data from a local database to the global data.

On the other hand, mapping maintenance is defined as the detection as well as correction of mapping inconsistencies that are resulting from schema evolution. It has been observed that Source schemas may go through structural or semantic changes that invalidate mappings.

4.4. DATA SECURITY

Figure 4.2: Data security helps in protecting the data, such as those available in the database.

Source: Image by Pixabay.

Data security is considered as a large subject. This is because it touches every activity of an information system. Data security introduces concepts and techniques which can be regarded as security measures. For instance, the process of recovery, whether it is from partial or total failure, should be considered as having a security dimension.

It has been observed that nearly all the work on concurrency is directed at the other aspect of security. Here, the main discussion is about the focusing on database security rather than security in general. Different principles of security theory and various practice in relevance with database security are important and must be discussed.

Also, there are technical aspects of security in spite of the big picture.

The second part is about logical access control in SQL database.

- Discretionary access control (DAC) is defined as a form of security access control that grants or restricts the access to an object through an access policy that is determined by an object's owner group and/or subjects. DAC mechanism controls are described by user identification with supplied credentials at the time of authentication, like username and password. DACs are discretionary. This is because the subject (owner) can transfer the information access or the authenticated objects to the other users. In other terms, object access privileges are determined by the owner.

UNIX file mode is a typical example of DAC. This defines the write, read, and execute permissions in each of the three bits for every single user, group, and others.

DAC attributes consists of:

- User may transfer the ownership of the object to the other user (s);
- User may also determine the access type of another users;
- Authorization failures restrict user access after a number of attempts;
- Unauthorized users are blind to object characteristics, such as file size, file name and directory path; and
- Object access is determined during access control list (ACL) authorization. This is based on user identification and/or group membership.

There are some limitations in DAC. There is one problem that is a malicious user can have access to the unauthorized data through an authorized user. For example, there is a user A who is having an authorized access to relations R and S and there is one user B who has authorized access to relation S only. If B in some way manages to modify an application program that is used by the user A so it writes R data into S, then the user B can read unauthorized data without violating authorization rules.

This problem is answered by multilevel access control and further it enhances the security by describing different security levels for both subjects as well as data objects. In addition to it, multilevel access control in databases is based on the well-known Bell and Lapaduda model that is designed for operating system security (Bell and Lapuda, 1976).

In this model, subjects are the processes that are acting on the behalf of a user; a process has a security level also known as clearance. This is derived from the user. In its simplest form, the security levels are Top Secret (T S), Confidential (C), Secret (S), and Unclassified (U), and ordered as T S > S > C > U, where ">" means "more secure." The access in read and write modes by subjects is constrained by two simple rules:

- A subject S is allowed to write an object of security level l only if class (S) $\leq$ l

- A subject S is allowed to read an object of security level l only if level (S) ≥ l.

4.4.1. Distributed Access Control

In addition to this, the issues with the access control in a distributed environment stem from the fact that the objects and the subjects are distributed and the messages with the sensitive data can be read through the users that don't have the authority. These issues are authentication of remote user, management of the discretionary access rule, management of the views and of the user groups, and enforcing the multilevel access control.

The authentication of the remote user is very important, from the time of any site of a distributed Data Base Management System may accept the programs initiated, and the authorized, at remote sites. In order to prevent the remote access with the help of users that are not authorized or the applications (for example, from a site that is not the part of the distributed DBMS), users must also be identified and authenticated at the accessed site.

In addition to this, as an alternative to using a password that could be acquired from sniffing the messages, encrypted certificates could be used.

4.4.2. Transaction Concept

A transaction is a unit of program implementation that accesses and perhaps updates the several numbers of data items. A transaction makes it easier with respect to the frequency of preserving the changes. In this way, a transaction, alters the database from an initial consistent state to the next consistent state with the help of a set to operation which are applied on the data items.

A transaction is consisting of the operations which are enclosed with the help of begin transaction and end transaction statements. States of Transaction A will go through the several numbers of states through the course of its implementation that are mentioned below:

- Active: A transaction is in active state through the course of its implementation;
- Partially committed: A transaction comes to partially committed state, when the final statement is implemented;
- Failed: A failed state is reached after the discovery that the normal implementation can no longer proceed;

- Aborted: The implementation of the transaction has failed, and this implementation does not have any kind of impact on the initial consistent state of the database; and
- Committed: The Transaction is said to be committed if it has successfully completed its implementation.

4.4.3. ACID Properties

A DBMS must maintain the four properties of the transaction to make sure the integrity of the data. These four properties are mentioned below:

- Atomicity: Either all of the operations of the transaction are carried out or none of them carried out. The transactions that are not completed should not have any kind of the impact on the state of the database in case of failures.
- Consistency: Each and every transaction in isolation with no concurrent implementation of other transaction should preserve the consistency of the database.
- Isolation: This property ensures that to preserve the consistency, two operations that are conflicting (for instance, read, and write or write and write) on the same data item with the help of two various transactions are not permitted. The isolation property is enforced with the help of a concurrency control mechanism or serialization mechanism.
- Durability: After the effective completion of the transaction its impact should persist even if the system fails before all the alterations are reflected on the disks.

The regularity of the transactions has to be made sure with the help of the users. The next state of the database is the consistent only if the previous state was consistent or regular. A transaction takes it for granted that it always works on the consistent database and it also makes sure that it will produce a regular or frequent database state.

The isolation property is accomplished with the help of making sure that, never the less, the actions of various transactions might be interleaved, the net impact is quite similar in order to implement all the transactions one after the other in some sort of serial order. The net impact of the concurrent execution of two transactions T1 and T2 is guaranteed to be correspondent in order to executing the T1 followed by implementing the T2 or implementing the Transaction 2 (T2) followed by the implementation of Transaction 1 (T1).

The atomicity of the transaction is making sure with the help of undoing the action of the incomplete transactions. With respect to this, a log consisting of all writes to the database is maintained with the help of DBMS. The log is also very helpful in order to make sure the durability.

A system failure can take place before the updates made with the help of the transaction are written to disk permanently. In this context, the log is used to remember and restore these kinds of alterations when the system restarts.

4.5. TYPES OF TRANSACTIONS

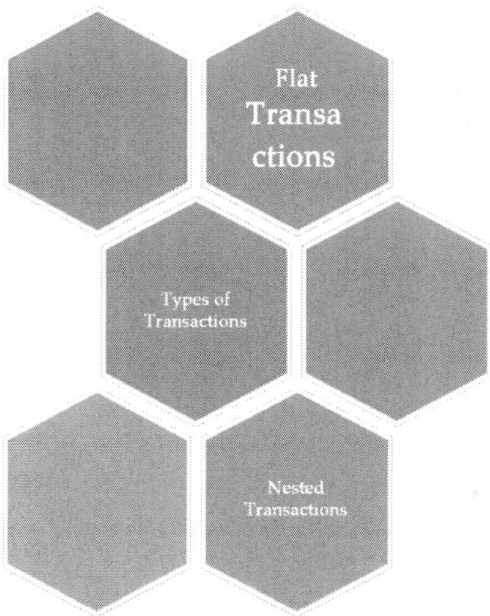

Figure 4.3: Different types of transactions.

There are a number of transaction models that have been suggested in literature, each being adequate for a class of applications. The fundamental problem of providing "ACID" usually remains, but the techniques and algorithms which are used to solve them may be substantially different. In some scenarios, several aspects of ACID requirements are lenient, fixing some problems and adding new ones (Figure 4.3).

4.5.1. Flat Transactions

Flat transactions have a single start point (known as Begin transaction) and a single termination point (known as End transaction). Most of the examples that are discussed in this, are of this type. Almost all transaction management work in databases has been focused on flat transactions. This model will also be major area of focus in this chapter, even though there has also been discussion on management techniques for other transaction types, where appropriate.

4.5.2. Nested Transactions

An alternative transaction model is to give permission to a transaction to embrace other transactions with their own commit and begin points. Such transactions can be defined as a nested transaction. These transactions that are fixed into another one is generally referred as sub transactions. It is generally seen that majority of the travel agents will make reservations for hotels and car rentals in addition to the flights

4.6. WORKFLOWS

Flat transactions model is comparatively simple and also carries short activities. However, they are considered less adequate for modeling longer and more elaborate activities. The major cause for the formation of the several nested transaction models discussed above. It has been argued that these extensions are not adequately powerful to model business activities: "after several decades of data processing, we have learned that we have not won the battle of modeling and automating complex enterprises" (MedinaMora et al., 1993).

In order to fulfill these needs, it is utmost important to propose more complex transaction models which are mixtures of both nested and open transactions. This is one of most important steps that should not be ignored in order to get the desired result. There are well-justified arguments for not calling these transactions, since they very rarely follow any of the ACID properties; a more appropriate name that has been projected is a workflow (Dogac et al., 1998b; Georgakopoulos et al., 1995).

4.7. INTEGRITY CONSTRAINTS IN DISTRIBUTED DATABASES

It has been observed that the distributed database systems have come up at the border of two areas. These two areas actually are in contrast to each other as far as the data processing is concerned: that are computer networks and database systems. The definition of the distributed databases is defined as a collection of logically interconnected databases. These interconnected databases are allocated in the computer network.

In this way, the distributed databases systems are not a simple collection of tables to be stored in each network node in a separate manner. The tables should be interconnected logically in order to form the database. Also, the access to the tables in question should be attained using a common interface.

A most important characteristic that is associated to the databases is integrity. Conserving the data integrity is considered as a much more difficult job with respect to the heterogeneous distributed databases as compared to that of the homogeneous databases.

If the nodes in the distributed database are heterogeneous in nature, then it is the possibility that they become an issue. This could provide harm or it dangers the integrity of the distributed data. These are mentioned below:

- Challenges in specifying the global integrity constraints;
- Inconsistencies between the local integrity integration constraints; and
- inconsistencies between the local and the global integrity constraints.

It has been observed that the local integrity constraints can variate, or these constraints fluctuates in the case of heterogeneous distributed databases. Inconsistencies can also bring about problems, and this is particularly valid in the case of complicated queries. These queries are based on more than one database. The creation of the global integrity constraints can help in providing assistance in preventing the conflicts that are between the individual databases that are associated with more organizations.

It has been observed that these types of developments are not always easy to execute as they seen. These developments are not easy and also, these are not practically acceptable in order to change the organization structure. This is done in order to convert the distributed database into a consistent one. In addition to it, this can take into the direction towards inconsistencies between the local and the global constraints.

Then, the conflicts, according to the level of the central control. The priority is given to global integrity constraints if the control coming from the center is powerful. On the other hand, if the control coming from the center is not powerful, then the priority is given to the local integrity.

4.7.1. The Semantic Model for Integrity Constraints

The sematic model provided a means for the formal definition of the significance of the logical database. An interpretation with regard to a logical language is an evaluation (or it is more like attribution) between true as well as false with respect to each (that is defined) base atom or event.

In addition to it, it can also be written as a set. It has to be noted that any type of atom in the set is seen as true. Any kind of atom construction, on the other hand, that is not in the set is known as false. Any sentence that is built can receive an evaluation that is associated to the implementation. In addition to it, it maintains the true value, beyond the logical connectors as well as quantifiers.

4.8. DISTRIBUTED QUERY PROCESSING

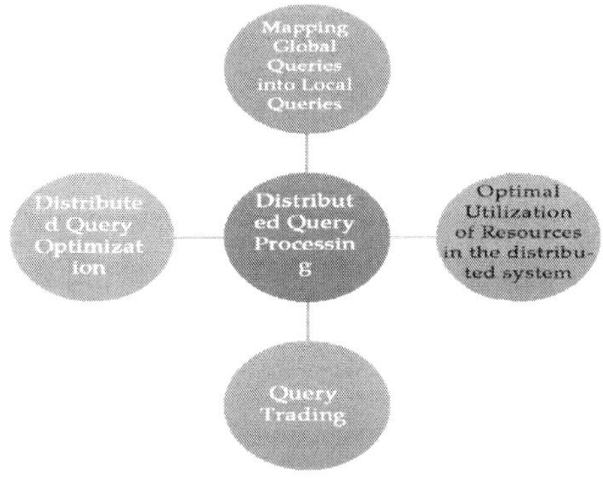

Figure 4.4: Distributed query processing.

The process of the distributed query processing is defined as the procedure of offering the correct or suitable answers to all the queries (this means mainly read operations on the large data sets) in a distributed environment. In this environment, the data is handled, or it is regulated at several numbers of locations with regards to a computer system (Figure 4.4).

The query processing is including the conversion of the high-level query (for instance, formulated in SQL) into the query execution plan (that includes the lower-query operators in some fluctuations of the relational algebra) all along with the implementation of the plan.

The main objective of the conversion or the transformation is to establish a plan. This developed plan is similar to the original query (as an outcome, it generates the similar result) and effective, that is, in order to lessen the utilization of resource like total costs or feedback time.

4.8.1. Mapping Global Queries into Local Queries

The entire procedure of mapping the global queries to local ones can be addressed as it is mentioned below:

- The tables that are required in a global query have fragments. These fragments are distributed all across the various numbers of locations. The local databases include the information that is only about the local data that is available at that point of time. The regulation of the sites makes use of the global data dictionary. This is done in order to gather the information about the distribution and, also reconstruct the global view from the fragments.
- The global optimizer runs the local queries at the sites where the fragments are stored, if there is no duplication or replication. On the other hand, the global optimizer chooses the site that is based on the communication cost, speed of the server, and load of the work, if there is any kind of duplicity or replication.
- The global optimizer produces, or it establishes a distributed implementation plan, in such a manner that, the smallest amount of the data transfer take place across the locations or sites. The implementation plan states the location of the fragments, the sequence in which the query steps is needed to be implemented and the process that take place in carrying out the intermediate outcomes.
- Optimization of the local queries takes place with the help of the servers of the local database. As a result, in the end, the local query is integrated with the help of the union operation in case of the horizontal fragments. Also, it joins operation with regards to the vertical fragments.

4.8.2. Distributed Query Optimization

The procedure of the distributed query optimization requires the assessment or the evaluation of huge number of query tress. Each of these makes or develops the required or needed results of a query. This is particularly because of the presence of the huge amount of the duplicate or replicates data along with the fragmented data.

In this way, the main purpose is to find out an optimal solution. This solution works as an alternative to the best possible solution.

The major problem with respect to the optimization of the query are given below:

- Optimal use of resources in the distributed system;
- Decrement of the solution space of the query; and
- Trading of the Query.

4.8.3. Optimal Utilization of Resources in the Distributed System

A distributed system includes numbers of database servers in various numbers of locations in order to perform all the operations that are associated or linked with the query. In addition to it, there are various numbers of approaches or methodologies that are used for the optimal utilization of resource. These are given below:

- **Operation Shipping**: The operation is performed at the location where the data is being stored and it is not run at the location of the client, with respect to the shipping. Then, the outcomes are carried away and these outcomes are transferred to the location of the client. This is appropriate with respect to the operations where the operands are present at the same location. For example, the operation of select and project.
- **Data Shipping**: The fragments of the data are carried away to the server of the database, where the implementation of operations takes place, with respect to the data shipping. This is utilized in operations, where the operands are situated at various numbers of different locations.

In addition to it, this is also suitable with respect to the systems, where the costs of communication are relatively low. Also, in this, the local processors are much then the server of the client.

- **Hybrid Shipping**: In the hybrid shipping, hybrid shipping is defined as the combination of the data as well as the operation shipping. In addition to it, the fragments of the data are being transferred to those processors that work on high speeds, where the operations are implemented. Then, the results are transferred to the location of the client.

4.8.4. Query Trading

While referring to the query trading algorithm with respect to the distributed database systems, the location of controlling or client for a distributed query is known as the buyer. On the other hand, the sites where the local queries implement are called sellers. The buyers formulate or establishes various numbers of alternatives in order to choose the sellers and in order to reconstruct the global outcomes. The main aim of the buyer is to achieve the optimal cost.

The algorithm started with the buyer, when buyer distributes the sub-queries to the location of the seller. The optimal plan is established with the help of local optimized query plans. These query plans are proposed with the help of sellers that are integrated with the communication cost. This is done in order to reconstruct the final result. The query is ready to implement once the global optimal plan is developed.

4.9. CONCLUSION

In the domain of database management, it is very important to understand the concept of Distributed database systems. The distributed database systems are the kind of database systems that are interconnected at multiple points with different logic. It is very important to understand the concept of Distributed database designs.

Various architectural models of distributed database systems are discussed in this chapter that explains how distributed database systems are helpful in the database management. One of the most important aspect of Database management is Schema mapping.

This explains the process with which the data from various local databases are linked to the target or the schema. This entire process of schema mapping is very significant as it explicitly extracts the data from various databases and then translates the data for populating it in various DWs.

There are different types of transaction models that are used in managing the distributed database systems. The major types of transaction models in the database systems are Flat transactions and Nested transactions. Nested transactions hold more importance as they allow different transactions, known as sub-transactions, to be included in other transactions within specific starting and ending points.

Distributed query processing explains the process of answering different queries in a distributed database system. This is very important as the distributed database systems are handled from different points. So, in order to resolve or answer a particular query, it is very necessary to have distributed query processing systems which allows proper resolution of the queries.

REFERENCES

1. Database Security. (n.d.). [ebook] pp.4–25. Available at: https://www.cs.uct.ac.za/mit_notes/database/pdfs/chp12.pdf (accessed on 1 June 2020).
2. Moldovan, G., & Valeanu, M., (2006). *Integrity Constraints in Distributed Databases*. 11th ed. [ebook] Alba Iulia: Acta Universitatis Apulensis. Available at: https://www.academia.edu/20051723/INTEGRITY_CONSTRAINTS_IN_DISTRIBUTED_DATABASES (accessed on 1 June 2020).
3. Overview of Transaction Management. (n.d.). [ebook] shodhganga, pp. 20–46. Available at: https://shodhganga.inflibnet.ac.in/bitstream/10603/24896/8/08_chapter%202.pdf (accessed on 1 June 2020).
4. Ozsu, M., & Valduriez, P., (2020). *Principles of Distributed Database Systems* (3rd edn.) [ebook] Springer. Available at: http://lib.sgu.edu.vn:84/dspace/bitstream/TTHLDHSG/2980/1/Principles%20Of%20Distributed%20Database%20Systems%20%20-%20%20M.%20Tamer%20Ozsu,%20Patrick%20Valduriez.pdf (accessed on 1 June 2020).
5. Risch, T., Canli, T., Khokhar, A., Yang, J., Munagala, K., Silberstein, A., Chrysanthis, P., (2009). Distributed query processing. *Encyclopedia of Database Systems*, [online] pp. 912–917. Available at: https://link.springer.com/referenceworkentry/10.1007%2F978-0-387-39940-9_704 (accessed on 1 June 2020).
6. Tutorialspoint.com. (n.d.). *Query Optimization in Distributed Systems-Tutorialspoint*. [online] Available at: https://www.tutorialspoint.com/distributed_dbms/distributed_dbms_query_optimization_distributed_systems.htm (accessed on 1 June 2020).
7. Valduriez, P., (n.d.). *Principles of Distributed Data Management in 2020?* p. 1. [ebook] arxiv.org/. Available at: https://arxiv.org/ftp/arxiv/papers/1111/1111.2852.pdf (accessed on 1 June 2020).

CHAPTER 5

Distributed Objects Database Management

CONTENTS

5.1. Database And Database Management System 114
5.2. Database Schemas 115
5.3. Different Kinds of Systems 116
5.4. Distributed Dbms 117
5.5. Object-Oriented Database Management System 123
5.6. Popular Object Databases 129
5.7. Object Management Process, Issues, and Application Examples 133
5.8. Conclusion 142
References 143

In this chapter, the concept of distributed objects database management has been discussed in this chapter. The database schemas has also been discussed in detail in chapter. There is also a discussion about types of DBMS in this chapter.

In this chapter there is a detailed discussion about distributed DBMS. The object data model, and its structure aspects and its operations has also been discussed in this chapter. The ODBMS database language has also been discussed in detail.

The object-oriented database management system (DBMS), its features, has also been discussed in this chapter. In this chapter, the advantages of object-oriented databases (OODB), the object-oriented databases and its uses, the components of object-oriented data model has also been discussed. The advantages and drawbacks of object databases has also been discussed in this chapter.

There are some popular object databases that has been described here in detail. In this chapter, the object management process, issues, and application examples has been discussed in detail in this chapter.

5.1. DATABASE AND DATABASE MANAGEMENT SYSTEM

The database is an ordered collection of the related data built for a particular purpose. The database can be organized as a set of multiple tables, where a table represents an element or entity of the real world. Every table has many different fields that reflects the distinctive features of the entity.

For example, the company database may also contain, for example, tables for projects, employees, departments, products, and financial records. The Name, Company Id, Date of Joining and other details might come in the fields in the Employee table.

The data base management system is a set of programs that allow a database to be created and maintained. The software package which allows data to be defined, constructed, manipulated, and shared in a database is available as DBMS. The definition of a database contains a description of the structure of a database.

A database construction includes the physical storing of the data in any storage medium. The manipulation is defined as the retrieval of data base information, updating of the database and reports generation. The data sharing makes it easier for different users or programs to access the data.

Examples of DBMS Application Areas

- Automatic Teller Machines;
- Train Reservation System;
- Employee Management System; and
- Student Information System

The Examples of DBMS Packages

- dBASE;
- FoxPro;
- PostgreSQL;
- MySQL;
- Oracle; and
- SQL Server, etc.

5.2. DATABASE SCHEMAS

The database schema is a representation of the database that is specified at the time of the database design, and rare alterations can be carried out later in it.

It determines the structure of the data the relationships between them, and the related constraints with them.

The databases are often depicted through the architecture of three schemas or by ANSISPARC architecture. This architecture has the purpose of separating the user application from the physical database (Figure 5.1)

The three levels are:

- **Internal Level having Internal Schema:** It explains the database's physical structure, details of internal storage, and access paths for the database.
- **Conceptual Level Having Conceptual Schema:** It describes the layout of the entire database while hiding the information of the physical storage of data. This demonstrates the entities, attributes, operations, and relationships, with their data types and constraints.

- **External or View Level having External Schemas or Views:** It defines the section of the database specific to a particular user or group of users while the rest of the database is hidden.

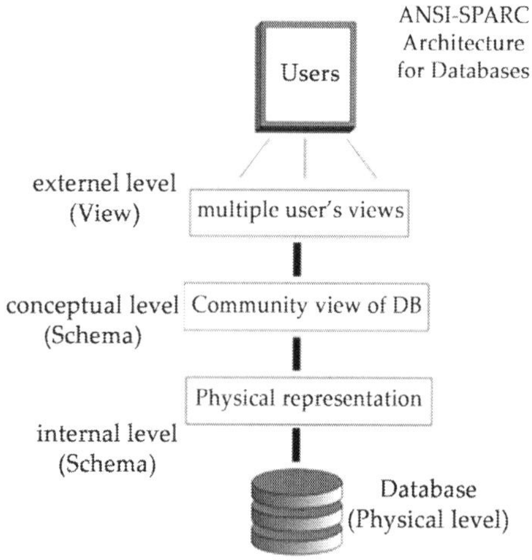

Figure 5.1:ANSI-SPARC DB model.

Sources: Image by Wikimedia.

5.3. DIFFERENT KINDS OF SYSTEMS

There Are Four Types Of DBMS.

- Hierarchical DBMS;
- Relational DBMS;
- Network DNMS; and
- Object Oriented DBMS.

Three of these DBMSs have already been explained in the previous chapters and Relational DBMS has been discussed in detail too. The Objected Oriented DBMSs is explained in the following text.

5.3.1. Object Oriented DBMS

The DBMS that is Object-oriented originates from the model of object-oriented programming paradigm. These are useful in both portraying stable data as stored in databases, as well as transient data as found in executing programs. They use small elements, called objects that are reusable.

Every object contains a part of the data and a series of operations that work with the data. Instead of being stored in relational table models, the object and its attributes are accessed through pointers.

5.4. DISTRIBUTED DBMS

A distributed database is a collection of interconnected databases spread over the network of computers on the internet. A Distributed DBMS manages the distributed database and provides frameworks for accountability of users across the databases.

The data is deliberately distributed between multiple nodes in these systems, so that all the computing resources in the organization can be efficiently utilized.

5.4.1. Object Data Model

There are many alternative data models have been proposed over the past two decades, including the entity-relationship (E-R) data model, the semantic data model, and the functional data model, etc. The goal in all of these efforts was to provide a more natural and richer way to represent the semantics of complex application domains.

There are many research papers explaining the data model of objects like [MARI88] and [BANE87] have been published in the past. Till now there is no complete consensus on the objects data model.

5.4.2. Structural Aspects of the Object Data Model

The objects, classes, and inheritance are the foundation of the object data model's structural aspects.

In general, it means the following

- Objects are simple entities that have data structures and operations.
- Each object has an object ID which is a unique identifier, which is provided by the system.
- Classes define generic types of objects. The descriptions of class are utilized to create individual objects, or instances of classes. All the objects are members of the class.
- Classes are associated by inheritance. The classes could be connected by super class or subclass relationships in order to form hierarchies of classes.

effort during the development of design applications. This effort might last a few hours, or even days. In lengthy sequences of transactions taking place in long design sessions involving multiple collaborating participants, large numbers of objects (possibly composite objects) that constitute the design may be modified.

In such cases, individual transactions may be expected to communicate with each other, or even interact. The Strict serialization criteria developed, based on locking protocols, need to be relaxed and replaced by more versatile, specific design criteria. This more versatile framework could ensure accuracy of the updated information, but also allow for a more random mix of transactions.

- **Support for Versioning:** The version management is a system for monitoring and documenting changes made to the data over time. The version management systems are important to document the history of the changes in design. A versioned object may have several alternate states, each of which, over time, corresponds to a distinct version of the object.

The version management system monitors successors and predecessors of the models. Once objects that comprise a portion of the design are recovered, the device must maintain accurate and compatible versions of those objects.

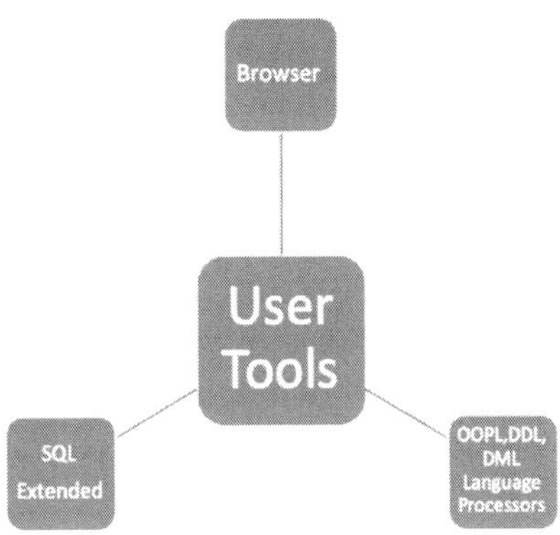

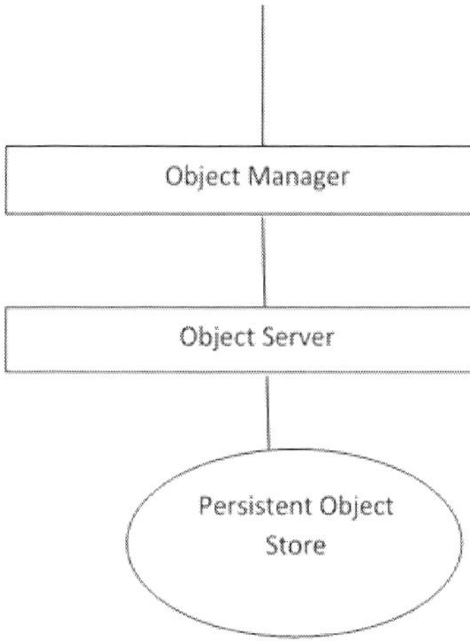

Figure 5.2: Overall architecture Of ODBMS.

5.5. OBJECT-ORIENTED DATABASE MANAGEMENT SYSTEM

The object-oriented database management system (OODBMS), often shortened to ODBMS for object database management system, is a DBMS that supports data as object modeling and its development. This requires some type of support for classes of objects, and the inheritance by subclasses and their artifacts of class properties and methods.

There is no universally accepted standard about what constitutes an OODBMS, though in 2001 the Object Data Management Group (ODMG) stated the Object Data Standard ODMG 3.0 that defines both an object model and requirements for object description and query. The group has dissolved after that.

The Data database systems, Not Only SQL (NoSQL) are currently a popular alternative to the database object. Although they are missing all of a true ODBMS features, NoSQL document databases provide key-based access to semi-structured data as records, usually using JavaScript Object Notation (JSON).

Motivated by the widespread use of object-oriented programming languages, object-oriented database (OODB) management systems often referred to as object databases were developed in the 1980s. The aim was to be able to store the objects easily in a database in a manner that correlates to their representation in a programming language, without any need for conversion or decomposition. Additionally, the relationships between the objects should also be preserved in the database. For example, Inheritance.

Therefore, an object-oriented DBMS implements an object-oriented data model of classes (the object scheme), properties, and methods. An object is always handled in its entirety. For example, this implies that the insertion of an object, that would possibly be stored in several tables in a relational system, will be performed automatically as one atomic transaction-without the application program taking any action. They can also interpret an entity as a single operation and without complex joining. The object databases also employ their own SQL-like query languages for manipulation of objects.

In recent times, certain object-oriented features have been applied to the classic relational DBMSs, like the user-defined data types and structured attributes. Some of those extensions within SQL were even standardized.

This reality and the convenient features, resources, and frameworks now available for storing objects into relational databases (like the Hibernate or JPA), hinders the widespread use of object-oriented systems.

The most popular examples are:

- Matisse;
- Intersystem Cache;
- Object Store;
- Versant Object Database; and
- Db4o.

5.5.1. Features of an ODBMS

The Malcolm Atkinson and others in the research paper titled The OODB Manifesto, described an OODBMS as-

The OODB system must meet two criteria: it should be a DBMS, and it should be an object-oriented system; i.e., it should be compatible with the current crop of object-oriented programming languages to the extent possible.

The first criteria translates into five features:

- Durability;
- Secondary storage management;
- Flexibility;

- Recovery; and
- A facility for ad hoc queries.

The second translates into eight characteristics:

- Complex structures;
- Identification of objects;
- Encapsulation;
- Forms or classes;
- Inheritance;
- Overriding combined with late binding; and
- Extensibility and completeness of computations.

5.5.2. RDBMS vs. ODBMS

The most commonly used form of DBMS is currently the Relational Database Management Systems (RDBMS). Most IT professionals understand well the relational abstraction of the rows and columns accessed using Structured Query Language (SQL).

On the other hand, object database systems could be better suited for the storage and manipulation of complex data relationships. In applications, accessing data with many relationships stored over many tables in an RDBMS can be more difficult than accessing the data as an object in an ODBMS.

In addition, many developers use object-oriented programming (OOP) languages to develop applications like the Java, C++, Python, and others. The use of an RDBMS to store and retrieve objects involves conversions from several relational database tables between complex objects and rows. The object-relational mapping (ORM) software may make this effort easier, but do not remove the mapping overhead.

The benefit of ODBMS is the absence of impedance mismatch when writing applications using the OOP approach; that is, the software handles and operates with objects instead of rows of data to be merged into an entity.

Most RDBMS vendors have expanded their products to the ORDBMS (Object-relative Database Management System). Superimposing such object-oriented principles on relational databases does not, of course, provide an ODBMS with the full feature set.

5.5.3. The Advantages of Object-Oriented Databases

The object-oriented database (OODB) or object-oriented database management system (OODBMS) is an object-oriented programming (OOP) based database. The data is represented and stored in the object form. The object databases or object-oriented management systems is also called OODBMS.

A Data storage is indeed a database. A DBMS is a software system used to administer databases. There are several types of DBMSs exist, like the hierarchical, network, relational, object-oriented, graph, and document.

5.5.4. Object-Oriented Database and Its Uses

The objects in object-oriented programming form the basis of object database management systems (ODBMS). In the OOP, an entity is represented as an object, and in memory objects are stored. Such objects have members that includes fields, properties, and methods.

The objects also have a life cycle that involves an object being created, an object being used, and an object being deleted. OOP has important features, encapsulation, inheritance, and polymorphism. There are many common OOP languages today, like the C++, Java, C#, Ruby, Python, JavaScript, Perl, etc.

Originated in 1985, the concept of object databases has become common today for various common OOP languages such as C++, Java, C#, Smalltalk, and LISP. Common examples are Gemstone uses the Smalltalk, Gbase uses the LISP and Vbase uses the COP.

The object databases are widely used in applications that needs high performance calculations and faster outcomes. There are some of the general applications using the object databases are real-time systems, 3D modeling architecture and engineering, telecommunications, and scientific products, molecular science, and astronomy.

5.5.5. Components of Object-Oriented Data Model

The OODBMS is focused on three main components, mainly: structure of the object, classes of the object, and identity of the object. Those are explained as following

1. **Object Structure:** An object's structure refers to the properties which make up an object. These attributes of an entity are called an attribute. Thus, an object is an entity of the real world with

some attributes which make up the structure of an object. An object also encapsulates the application code into a single unit that in turn provides data abstraction by hiding user details about the implementation.

The structure of an object is further composed of three component types: messages, methods, and variables. These are listed as following

- **Messages:** A message offers an interface, which serves as a means of communication between an entity and the world outside.

A message can be of two types

1. Read-only message: If the method invoked does not modify a variable's value, then the message invoking is said to be a read-only message.
2. Update message: If the method invoked changes a variable's value then the message invoking is said to be an update message.

- **Methods:** The body of code that is executed is recognized as a method when a message is transmitted. Each time as the process is executed, a value returns as output.

A method can be of two types

1. Read-only method: If a method does not influence a variable's value, then it is called read-only method.
2. Update-method: When a variable's value changes by a process, it is called an update method.

- Variables: The data of an object is stored in it the data stored in the variables renders the object differentiable from each other.

2. Object Classes

An object which is an entity of the real world is an example of a class. They must therefore first define a class and then make the objects that differ in the values they store but share the same definition of class. The objects in turn correspond to different messages and variables that are stored within it.

An OODBMS also thoroughly supports inheritance, as there may be several classes with similar methods, variables, and messages in a database. The definition of class hierarchy is thus retained to represent the similarities between different classes.

The definition of encapsulation which is the hiding of data or information is also endorsed by the model of object-oriented data. And, apart from the built-in data types like char, int, float, this data model also provides the abstract data type facility. ADT's are the types of data identified by the user that carry the values within it and may also have methods attached to it.

Thus, OODBMS provides its users with various facilities, both built-in and user-defined. This combines the properties of an object-oriented data model with a DBMS and embraces the definition of programming paradigms such as classes and objects together with support for other principles such as encapsulation, inheritance, and the user-defined abstract data types (ADTs).

5.5.6. Advantages of Object Databases

The persistent storage to objects is given by ODBMS. Imagine creating and saving items in your program as they are in a database and reading them back from the database.

The data of the system is stored in rows and columns in a standard relational database. In order to store and read the data and transform it into memory program objects needs reading data, loading data into objects, and storing it into memory.

The object databases render objects indefinitely immutable. Objects may be preserved for ever in permanent storage.

The layer of object-relational mapping exists in typical RDBMS which maps database schemes with objects in code. Reading and mapping data from an object to the object database is direct without any API or QR method. Thus, faster access to data and better performance.

Few databases of objects can be used in many different languages. For example, the Gemstone database supports programming languages such as C++, Smalltalk, and Java.

5.5.7. Drawbacks of Object Databases

- The objects database are not as famous as RDBMS. The developers of object Database are hard to find;
- The object databases are not supported by many programming languages;
- RDBMS has SQL as the default query language. Databases of objects do not have a standard; and
- Databases on artifacts are hard for non-programmers to understand.

5.6. POPULAR OBJECT DATABASES

The list of some of the popular object databases and their features.

5.6.1. Cache

Cache by intersystem's is a high-performance object database. Cache database engine is a collection of services that include data storage, concurrency management, transaction management, and process management. One may think of the Cache engine as a powerful toolkit for databases.

Cache is a fully functional relational database, too. All of the data in a Cache database accessible as true relational tables and can be queried and updated using standard SQL through ODBC, JDBC, or object methods. One of the fastest, most efficient, and most scalable relational database is Cache.

Cache offers the following features:

- The capability to model data as objects each with automatically generated and synchronized native relational representation while removing both the impedance mismatch between databases and object-oriented application environments and the difficulty of relational modeling;
- The easier, object-based concurrency model;
- User-defined data types;
- The capacity to take advantage of methods and inheritance, like polymorphism, inside the database engine;
- Object-extensions for SQL to manage object identification and relationships;
- The ability to intermix SQL and user-based access within a single application, utilizing both for what they are best suited for; and
- The Control of the physical layout and clustering used to store data in a way to achieve maximum performance of applications.

Cache offers a wide range of tools that includes:

- Object Script, the language in which most of Cache is written;
- Native SQL, Multi Value, and Basic implementations;
- A well-developed, integrated security model;
- A suite of technologies and resources that provide rapid development for database and web applications;

- Support for native, object-based XML and web services;
- Support for devices like the files, TCP/IP, printers;
- Automatic interoperability through Java, JDBC, ActiveX, NET, C++, ODBC, XML, SOAP, Perl, Python, and more;
- Support for common Internet protocols POP3, SMTP, MIME, FTP, and so on;
- A flexible app interface for your end users;
- Unstructured data analysis support;
- The Business Intelligence (BI) support; and
- Built-in testing facilities.

5.6.2. Concept Base

The ConceptBase.cc is an object-oriented, multi-user deductive database system (data, class, meta class, meta-meta class, etc.) which makes it a powerful tool for the meta modeling and engineering of custom modeling languages.

Accompanying the device is a highly configurable graphical user interface that builds on the ConceptBase.cc server's logic-based functions.

The Concept Base Team at University of Skovde (HIS) and the University Of Aachen (RWTH) has developed the ConceptBase.cc. For Linux, Windows, and Mac OS-X, ConceptBase.cc is available. There is also a pre-configured virtual appliance that contains the executable system plus its sources plus the software to compile them. The machine is licensed under FreeBSD-style for distribution.

5.6.3. Db4o

Db4o is the largest Java and.NET open-source object database in the world. Leveraging the fast-native object persistence, ACID transactions, query-by-example, S.O.D.A object query API, Small size, automatic class schema evolution.

5.6.4. Object DB Object Database

The Object DB is an efficient, object-oriented data base management (ODBMS). It's lightweight, reliable, user friendly and extremely fast. The Object DB offers all standard data base management services storage and retrieval, transactions, lock management, query processing, etc. but in a way that encourages development and speeds up applications.

The important features of object DB object database are:

- The Java Object-Oriented Database Management System (ODBMS) 100% pure;
- No proprietary API-administered by standard Java APIs only (JPA 2/JDO 2);
- Extremely quick-quicker than any other JPA/JDO product;
- Ideal for database files ranging from kilobytes to terabytes;
- Promotes both Embedded mode and Client-Server mode;
- JAR single, without external dependency;
- Stored as a single file in the database;
- Basic expertise in querying and indexing;
- Active in multiuser environments with heavy loads;
- Can be easily embedded into applications of any type and size; and
- Tested with Tomcat, Jetty, Glassfish, and JBoss and Spring.

5.6.5. Object Database

Object database (ODBPP) is an object-oriented, embeddable database designed for server applications requiring minimal external service. It is written in C++ as an ISAM level database in real time with the ability to auto recover from system crashes while preserving the integrity of the database.

5.6.6. Objectivity DB

- Objectivity DB is a distributed Object Database (ODBMS) which is scalable, high performance. The handling of complex data is extremely good, where there are many types of connections between objects and many variants.
- Objectivity DB runs on Linux, Mac OS X, UNIX (Oracle Solaris), or Windows processors running 32 or 64-bit.
- There are APIs such as C++, C#, Java, and Python.
- All combinations of platforms and languages are interoperable. For example, a C# program on Windows can read objects stored

by a program using C++ on Linux, and a Java program on Mac OS X.

- Objectivity DB generally runs on POSIX file systems, but for other storage resources there are plugins that can be changed.
- Objectivity DB software programs can be designed to run on a stand-alone desktop, networked workgroups, large clusters, or in grids or clouds with no computer code changes.

5.6.7. Object Store

The enterprise object-oriented database management system for C++ and Java is Object Store.

Object Store provides several performance improvements by removing the middleware requirement for mapping and transforming application objects into flat relational rows by directly persisting objects inside an application in an object store.

The Object Store removes the need to flatten complex data for consumption in the application logic through and the overhead of using a translation layer that transforms complex objects into flat objects, dramatically improving performance and often entirely eliminating the need to manage a relational database system.

The Object Store is OO storage that integrates directly with Java or C++ applications and treats memory and permanent storage as one-improving application logic efficiency while maintaining full compliance with ACID against transactional and distributed load.

5.6.8. Versant Object Database

The object database that continues to support persistence of native objects and is used for the development of complex and high-performance data management systems is defined as Versant Object-Oriented Database.

The important benefits are:

- Significantly lower total ownership cost;
- Real-time analytical performance;
- Cut development time by up to 40%;
- Big data management; and
- High availability.

5.6.9. Wakanda DB

The Wakanda DB is an object database and provides a native REST API to access interconnected Data Classes defined in Server-Side JavaScript. Wakanda DB is the server within Wakanda which includes a dedicated, but not mandatory, Ajax Framework, and a dedicated IDE.

5.6.10. Object-Relational Databases

The databases which support both object and relational database features are Object-relational database (ORD) or object-relational database management systems (ORDBMS). OR databases are relational DBMSs with object-oriented database model support. That implies the entities are defined as objects and classes, and OOP features like the inheritance are supported in database schemas and in the query language.

PostgreSQL is pure ORDBMS which is the most popular. Some popular databases also support objects that includes Microsoft SQL Server, Oracle, and IBM DB2, and can be regarded as ORDBMS.

5.7. OBJECT MANAGEMENT PROCESS, ISSUES, AND APPLICATION EXAMPLES

In general, an object might allude to an indivisible entity ranging from a small text file to a large volume multimedia file, depending on the application underlying it. In database systems, for example, these objects can be systematically classified in the form of text files, audio clips, graphic files, video clips ranging from small to large sizes, and can be cleverly indexed to support the faster retrieval. An object is thus an entity which is specified by its type and size.

In addition, certain objects may be changed, i.e., they might be edited, and meaning the size of such objects is a variable quantity. Therefore, in a network system, any program can allow the move of an object from one node to another that will eat varying network bandwidth.

An important issue that is called object management process (OMP) is handling the objects on a network system. They will introduce some OMP methodologies and some performance metrics which are widely used to measure these methodologies' performance.

Usually, this OMP involves:

1. Monitoring where exactly the original source of an object resides;
2. Taking decision on the number of copies of an object currently required;
3. Allowing copies to be transferred to another location on the network as required;
4. Maintaining continuity between existing copies transmitting multi-casting information on any changes to an object at any node to other relevant nodes.

These types of earlier mentioned issues results in the use of huge amounts of computing resources and might incur overheads based on the type of requests submitted to the system. They will examine each of these issues that includes an OMP and specifically quote some application domains in which each of these issues may be more relevant.

There are some words that are used in OMP literature: First, an algorithm called an object location algorithm undertakes the process by which the requested objects are discovered, selected, and delivered from neighboring sites. Therefore, when this algorithm is invoked, it locates the requested object and may be permitted to deliver the requested object to the desired site depending on the flexibility of its architecture.

Second, from the point of view of common sense, the provision of network-based services seems more cost-effective and quicker than any traditional types of services. For example, subscribing to a network-based, multimedia film-on-demand (MOD) service with a service provider may be cheaper than visiting a video rental store for compact disk video cassettes at any time.

These network-based services also offer complete versatility in enabling consumers to communicate with the system. Thus, multiple copies of an object are required to be injected or developed on a network so that access is quicker, and more requests can be served.

The replication of objects therefore takes an essential function within an OMP. However, replicating too many copies will result in additional overheads like the maintaining consistency between the copies (when objects can be edited), requiring efficient algorithms for object consistency to be designed.

The task of object consistency algorithms is to ensure consistency of each available copy of an object on the network. In the easier meaning, this could be based on a time-stamping technique in which an object's recency is measured using a timestamp and the object was fetched from there.

Ultimately, depending on the application under consideration, algorithms may be used to ensure consistency, broadcasting or multicasting. Mainly multicasting algorithms are primarily needed, as copies of the objects only exist in a few places.

Moreover, it may also be likely that traditional multicasting algorithms may need to be revamped to suit the current needs of the problem context. For example, if links are not accessible in a planned route between a source site and a destination site, an intermediate site may at that time instantly route the object through other best available paths.

Therefore, the underlying topology of the network might dynamically change with regard to resource availability constraints. Therefore, traditional multi-casting algorithms suitable for static case may not be directly applicable in OMP where dynamic changes in the topology of the network occur. While replication is needed, it is often due to several factors, depending on the underlying applications, where exactly a replication is necessary.

Less famous movies may not be repeated regularly in a MOD system and stored on the network, since the popularity profile may be demanding. Also, replication might be difficult when the available capacity (or network bandwidth) becomes a bottleneck.

Depending on the demand profile, some systems allow a fixed number of copies to exist at some vantage points. Therefore, replication problems are closely associated with resource availability issues. In some systems migration of objects may be an alternative solution for replication of objects.

In such instances, if resources are scarcely accessible and the original copies are few in number, an existing copy may be moved from its current site to any remote selected site instead of replicating the item in other locations.

Additionally, this method of migration method can be based on the importance of object at a location. For example, if an object is most required in a site j and there is a copy at a site I where this object is less in demand, then object can be allowed to migrate to site j.

Such crucial decisions on the movement of objects are also part of OMP. OMP thus, ultimately, means choosing the best possible algorithms for each problem in place for the current network setup, object demand profile, resource availability constraints.

The following four application domains which use the above mentioned OMP directly in relation to their needs and constraints.

1. Hierarchical Storage and Remote Memory Paging Systems;
2. Video-on-Reservation Systems;
3. World Wide Web or LAN Systems caching or storage;
4. Distributed Server Systems.

These application domains have been specifically chosen because the existence of the objects under consideration varies in each domain and imparts different types of constraints.

5.7.1. OMP in Hierarchical Memory and Remote Memory Paging Systems

The designing of methods to handle the available memory bandwidth and space efficiently also poses the difficult problems. From conventional to modern computer architectures, performance enhancement has been shown to be important when memory management task is done in an efficient manner.

The memory hierarchy was envisaged in traditional architectures to range from tiny registers to tapes and disks as a means of storage media. In this case, the concept of an object is dependent on the level in the memory hierarchy concerned.

At the CPU level, an object assumes a size of in bytes, at the cache level an object is of size represented in cache lines on the pages (usually byte blocks), at the main memory level an object is of size pages (many byte blocks), and finally at the disk level it could be large segments comprising several pages, depending on the memory management underlying it.

The OMP refers to the decisions to be made at this single level processor to enable easier and faster access from the memory system to the appropriate datum. Now, considering a three Level hierarchy as an example within a memory system, when a page request is created, it is first searched in the cache (because of its high access speeds) and then they assume they have a hit if it is found.

However, if a miss occurs (date not identified at the correct Level), then the next higher Level is accessed to look for the desired data and this process continues. As demonstrated in several textbooks and literature, it may be beneficial from the efficiency point of view to maintain some of the most frequently accessed items in the cache in the expectation of some near future requests for these objects.

However, when there is an error, a decision must be made on which object to be removed from the cache or at the stage currently being considered in order to provide space for the object being requested. The algorithms that enable replacement of these page objects within a hierarchy of a memory system are referred to as page replacement algorithms.

Some of the most common algorithms in this group include the least recently used (LRU), most frequently used (MFU), less frequently used (LFU), size-based LRU (S-LRU), etc., to mention a few. Therefore, as far as an OMP is concerned, the problems with developing replacement algorithms are at a single node or site level.

The migration and duplication of objects are not appropriate for consideration on a single processor system level. Moreover, later they will find out that these are the fundamental techniques that are useful when making migration or replication decisions in web-caching problems, even at system level that is between sites.

Although the techniques used to minimize latencies during processing in a single CPU device were effective following the hierarchy, the power provided by the advent of modern-day high-speed computers, combined with the high-speed interconnection media networking technology, was rarely fully utilized.

The hierarchical architecture of the memory system can be defined as:

(a) Shared main-memory architecture;
(b) Direct shared virtual memory (DSVM); and
(c) Remote caching architecture (RCA).

With the technological advancement in the computer hardware as in networking, the current trend is centered on using RAC as a means to improve overall system performance. RCA's key feature is that sites request (and receive) remote sites objects with a faster response time than even accessing their own local disks.

This reality is genuinely comprehensive, and an expanded virtual memory space can be seen as the system the major difference from shared main memory architectures is that the sites do not actually need the ability to read or write directly to remote memory locations. Alternatively, it was suggested in the literature that RCA could use DSVM as a platform.

This ensures that there is a virtual address allocated to a particular job that can either refer to a local or remote location. The local disk access is only triggered when the requested objects cannot be found elsewhere in the network. Therefore, in providing an extended virtual memory space, RCA has an excellent benefit and offers a very large virtual space for a single site.

5.7.2. Interoperability Issues

While work on interconnecting various DBMSs has been underway for over a decade, it is only recently that many of the difficult issues are being addressed.

It's difficult to provide solutions to interconnect various DBMSs.

- **Schema (or data model) Heterogeneity:** Not all heterogeneous software databases are represented by the same data model. Therefore, it is important to incorporate the various conceptual schemas. To do this, translators are being developed which turn the constructs of one data model into those of another.
- **Heterogeneity of Transaction Processing:** Different DBMSs may use different algorithms to process transactions. The work is geared towards integrating the different mechanisms for processing transactions. For example, techniques are being developed which incorporate mechanisms for locking, time stamping, and validation.
- It has been proposed that the notion of strict serializability for a heterogeneous setting may need to be sacrificed. That is perhaps one with a weaker form of serializability to deal with.
- **Heterogeneity of Query Processing:** The different DBMSs may use different query processing and optimization strategies. One of the areas of research here is creating a global cost model for the optimization of distributed queries.
- **Heterogeneity of Query Language:** Different DBMS will use different Query languages. Even if the DBMSs are based on the relation model, SQL, and the other Relational Calculus could be used. The efforts of Standardization to develop a standard language for the GUI are being carried out.
- **Heterogeneity Constraint:** The different DBMSs place various integrity constraints that are often inconsistent. For example, one DBMS may impose a restriction that all workers are expected to work for at least 40 hours while another DBMS may not enforce such a limit.

- **Semantic Heterogeneity:** The data for different components may be interpreted differently. For example, the address of the entity might mean just the country at one component while the number, street name, city name and country could be interpreted as another component. It has been acknowledged that it is very difficult to handle semantic heterogeneity.

5.7.3. Schema Transformation

Central to the design of DBMSs is the issue of data representation; the success of database systems thus depends in part on the extent to which data can be represented within a particular scheme. Most database systems are commonly tailored for a specific application where the data representation scheme used depends on the application.

The Users of a heterogeneous system are expected to learn a variety of data representation schemes if they have to access remote systems. Clearly such demands on the user are undesirable. Ideally the user should be expected to know one or perhaps two schemes to be effective. For example, the database at site 1 could be represented by a relational model (RM) and the database at site 2 could be represented by a network model.

The Schema integration then amounts to transforming the constructs of one data model into those of the other. An advantage of this method is that users do not do not have to know all the data representation schemes being utilized. They need only the details of one representation scheme.

The translator will perform the necessary transformations. A disadvantage of such an approach is the large number of translators that may be necessary in a heterogeneous environment which utilizes many data models. For example, if n different data models are utilized, then n**2 (n squared) translators will be required. This is not in general desirable.

A second method of interconnection is to utilize an intermediate representation scheme. A specific data representation scheme is translated into the intermediate representation scheme; then the intermediate representation scheme is translated into the second data representation scheme. In this method, for n different data models, only 2 x n translators are necessary. This intermediate representation scheme is usually called the generic representation scheme.

An object-oriented representation scheme is being proposed to serve as the generic representation scheme. Such a representation has the power to model structural as well as behavioral properties of entities. Furthermore, most of the constructs of the other data models can be transformed into constructs of object-oriented data models. The schema integration using an object-oriented approach in heterogeneous environment consists of relational DBMS and a network DBMS.

Since relational DBMSs dominate the marketplace, the assessment of the relationship between a RM and an object-oriented model is

Generating relations from an object-oriented data model is a two-step process. During the first step, the object model is transformed into a collection of intermediate relations. They call this intermediate relational data model to be a generic relational data model. The second step is to transform the constructs of the generic relational data model into those of a specific relational data model such as the one used by a commercial product.

They will describe the first step to point out the essential concepts. Classes may be mapped into one or more relations. Consider the class aircraft. This class has characteristics ID, Name, Group, and Mission. It has an instance object whose ID is loo0, Name is AAA, Group is 10, and Mission is PPP.

The object-IDs of the instances could be used for primary keys or a mapping could be provided between the object-IDS and the user generated primary keys if users are to access the relations directly.

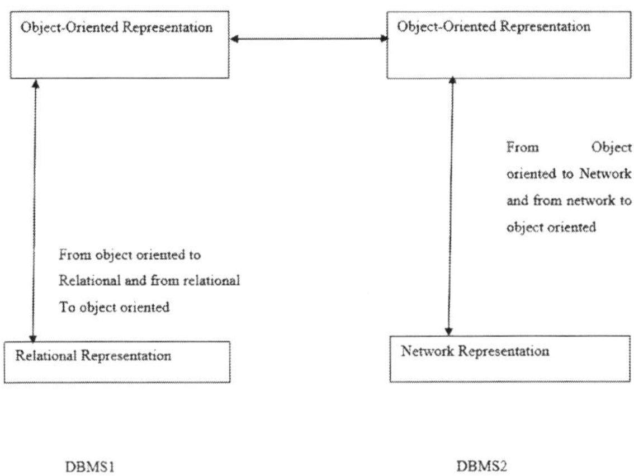

Figure 5.3: Schema integration.

5.7.4. Role of Object-Oriented Standards

The efforts in direction of Standardization are in the process for the types of object-oriented programming applications in the interoperability of heterogeneous database systems. The American National Standards Institute (ANSI) is designing requirements for a common-object model. Specifications are being formulated explicitly for the various object model constructs.

The ANSI's SQL committee is also proposing extensions to SQL to accommodate objects and types of multimedia data. Since SQL is a widely accepted language for defining and manipulating databases, one might expect the object extensions proposed for SQL to serve as the global data model in heterogeneous integration of databases.

Subsequently, the Object Data Management Group (ODMG). That is a consortium of several firms, has formulated standards for the object-oriented management of data. This group's proposed object model could also serve as the global data model.

CORBA by OMG shows great promise to incorporate heterogeneous database systems. The object model used, the Object Request Broker (ORB), and the Interface Definition Language (IDL) are three major components of CORBA.

The model of objects defines the interpretation of objects and the implementation of objects. The semantics of an object, form, requests, development, and destruction of artifacts, interfaces, operations, and attributes are defined as object semantics. The implementation of objects defines model of execution and model of construction.

The ORB essentially allows communication between client and server. The client is an individual performing an object operation, and the object implementation is the code and data actually executing the function.

The ORB includes all the methods for identifying the application object specification, preparing the implementation of the object to accept the request, and transmitting the details that make up the request. IDL is the language for defining the interfaces the client objects call and the implementations of the objects.

This language is descriptive. Notice that the clients and implementations of objects are not written in IDL. The subset of ANSI C++ is the IDL grammar with additional constructs to support the invocation mechanism for the process. The binding of IDL to C language has been specified. The other technique used by CORBA to incorporate heterogeneous database structures is to encapsulate the database servers as the server objects.

The clients of the database would be the client objects, and communication between clients and servers is achieved via the ORB. The goal is not to make changes to implementations of the client and server. The calls made by the client and the server must be converted into IDLs, however, so that communication can be made through the ORB (Figure 5.4).

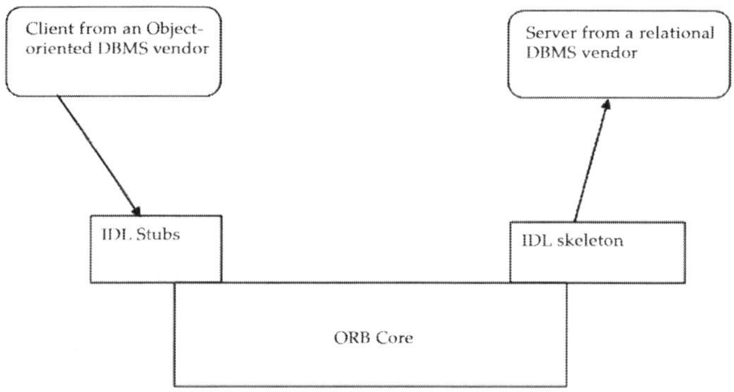

Figure 5.4: Interoperability using CORBA.

5.8. CONCLUSION

In every organization for proper functioning there is a requirement of the well-maintained database. The databases are used to be centralized in nature in the recent past. But with the rise of globalization, companies continue to diversify around the globe. In place of a central database, they might choose to spread data over local servers. Thus, the idea of Distributed Databases has arrived.

REFERENCES

1. C-sharpcorner.com. (2019). *What Are Object-Oriented Databases And Their Advantages?* [online] Available at: https://www.c-sharpcorner.com/article/what-are-object-oriented-databases-and-their-advantages2/ (accessed on 1 June 2020).
2. Dabrowski, C., Fong, E., & Yang, D., (1990). *Object Database Management Systems: Concepts and Features.* [ebook] National Institute of Standards and Technology, p. 2. Available at: https://www.govinfo.gov/content/pkg/GOVPUB-C13-c07e92e90356c95a30808e6c68bce72b/pdf/GOVPUB-C13-c07e92e90356c95a30808e6c68bce72b.pdf (accessed on 1 June 2020).
3. Db-engines.com. (n.d.). *Object oriented DBMS-DB-Engines Encyclopedia.* [online] Available at: https://db-engines.com/en/article/Object+oriented+DBMS (accessed on 1 June 2020).
4. GeeksforGeeks, (n.d.). Definition and Overview of ODBMS-GeeksforGeeks. [online] Available at: https://www.geeksforgeeks.org/definition-and-overview-of-odbms/ (accessed on 1 June 2020).
5. Rouse, M., (n.d.). *What is Object-Oriented Database Management* System (OODBMS)?-Definition from WhatIs.com. [online] SearchOracle. Available at: https://searchoracle.techtarget.com/definition/object-oriented-database-management-system (accessed on 1 June 2020).
6. Thuraisingham, B., (n.d.). *Application of Object-Oriented Technology for Integrating Heterogeneous Database Systems.* [ebook] p. 2. Available at: https://personal.utdallas.edu/~bxt043000/Publications/Conference-Papers/DM/C162_Application_of_Object-Oriented_Technology_for_Integrating_Heterogeneous_Database_Systems.pdf (accessed on 1 June 2020).
7. Tutorialspoint.com. (n.d.). *Distributed DBMS-Concepts-Tutorialspoint. [online*] Available at: https://www.tutorialspoint.com/distributed_dbms/distributed_dbms_concepts.htm (accessed on 1 June 2020).

CHAPTER 6

Client or Server Database Architecture

CONTENTS

6.1. Introduction 146

6.2. Working of Client-Server Architecture 148

6.3. Client And Server Characteristics 150

6.4. Advantages And Drawbacks Of Client-Server Architecture 151

6.5. Client-Server Architecture Types 152

6.6. Concept of Middleware In Client-Server Model 155

6.7. Thin Client/Server Model 157

6.8. Thick Client/Server Model 159

6.9. Services Of Client-Side In C/S Architecture 160

6.10. Services Of Server-Side In C/S Architecture 161

6.11. Remote Procedure Call 163

6.12. Security Of Client-Server Architecture 165

6.13. Conclusion 170

References 172

In a distributed database architecture, the client-server architecture is used for the purpose of information processing. The architecture has various aspects that support its working. The client and server present over the network communicate via a channel by the process of message passing.

These messages are transferred among clients and servers by which the clients request a service and the server responds with the result of the request. Initially, this chapter, the working, and characteristics of the client and server architecture have been described along with its advantages and drawbacks.

Further, its architecture types and different models of the client/server architecture have been described. The middleware is an essential aspect of the client/server architecture that has been elaborated along with its uses and types. In the end, the security issues are discussed which is a major cause of concern for the client-server architecture.

6.1. INTRODUCTION

Client-server architecture plays a very essential role in the distributed database environment as it allows the processing of the information from the client to the server. The clients are the remote processors that request service from the database which is a centralized server. In this architecture the server receives requests from clients and processes their request, then it compiles the result which is then sent to the client system.

There are various processes that a client can ask for from a server that may include data extraction and retrieval, data storage, etc. These activities are performed by the servers after they receive the request for the same. In a distributed database architecture, there are various computers that are connected over a network, and as per the requirements they might work as client, server, and at times both (Figure 6.1).

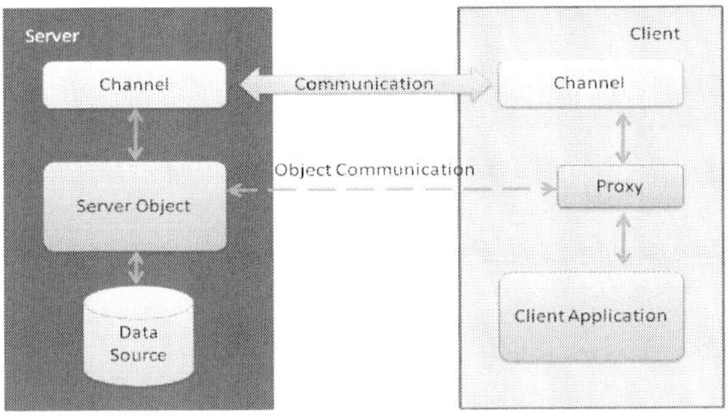

Figure 6.1: Client-server architecture.

Source: Image by Wikimedia.

There are two major frameworks for client-server architecture that are two-tier and three-tier architecture. As the clients and servers, both are on the same network and perform the services interchangeably, so in a two-tier architecture, there is a major disadvantage. The drawback of two-tier architecture is that in case the number of clients increases beyond a limit then it will become very complex for the server to handle the increased amount of request and it may behave inappropriately.

The request and response system are being used in the client-server architecture in which the client requests a service and the server responds to it by providing the client with the information that it requires. The protocol of communication that is being implemented in the client-server system is required to be the same so that the clients can efficiently communicate with the server.

In the client-server environment of computing priority-driven approach is used, as the server is not able to handle a lot of requests at once hence a limited number of clients can be served at one time. The major issue for this type of computing environment is that of denial of service (DoS) attack. This type of attack harms the efficiency of the system and also pose a major threat to the user data that is being transmitted over the network.

There are some issues that have been identified for this architecture that is in terms of communication protocol and network security. The attacks that can be performed on this architecture are DoS and Brute force attack. These attacks are performed when the data encryption approach is used for data security. The network transmission protocols are applied for security purpose but still, the intruders have various ways by which they can get access to the server.

The major issue that this architecture suffers from is in terms of its benefit that means, the services are divided to be performed in collaboration of clients and server over the network. This makes the system more open to vulnerable to get invoked by the hackers.

There are various instances when the client did not take proper steps for the security and left their system open to access by all, in these cases the clients are more responsible for their safety than the server or security protocols involved.

The security vulnerabilities are present in every system that works over the internet. The network over which the data is transmitted in a Client-Server architecture is connected to the internet and the hackers have the resources to get access to this data that is being transmitted over the internet-based network.

6.2. WORKING OF CLIENT-SERVER ARCHITECTURE

Since the advent of client-server architecture, it has become very popular among the business organizations that have continuous use of database services. The reason being the cost efficiency, the efficiency of processing applications and using resources to its full capacity. In simple terms, the efficiency factor is achieved by dividing the processes required to perform among the software of the client and server-side. This reduces the load on one system and the processes are completed efficiently.

The processes are not dependent on one another but the compatibility and cooperation among the processes are not compromised. When a service is requested by the client then it is completed with the cooperation of every independent process. This cooperation among the processing of the application is beneficial for the client-server architecture as it decreases the traffic over the network.

In a client-server architecture, there are three major components present namely, network, server, and client. All the data transmission process takes place over the network where the client requests a service and the server replies with the desired result. There are various connections present over a network in a system of client and server, these connections are the visual representation of a network.

The system implementation life cycle for the client-server architecture is provided in Table 6.1.

Table 6.1: System Installation Life Cycle

Phases of SILC	**Activities**
Planning	• System planning initiation • Data gathering • Current situation analysis • Existing system analysis • Requirement identification • Data architecture and application analysis • Technology platform analysis • Implementation plan preparation
Project Initiation	• Request for screen • Long-range system plan relationship identification • Project initiation • Next phase plan preparation
Architecture Definition	• Data gathering • Detailing of system requirement • Alternative solution conceptualization • Proposed architecture development • Vendor and product selection
Analysis	• Data acquisition • New application system logical model development • System requirements identification • External system design preparation
Design	• Preliminary design performance • Detailed design performance • System test designing • User aids designing • Conversation system designing
Development	• Development environment initiation • Code modules • User aids development • System test conduction

Implementation	• Contingency procedure development • Release and maintenance procedure development • User system training • Establishing production environment • Data conversion • Application system installation • Acceptance test support • Warranty support
Post-implementation strategies	• Maintenance and support initiation • Services • Communication and hardware configuration • Support software

Source: Table by Saintangelos

6.3. CLIENT AND SERVER CHARACTERISTICS

In order to complete a task over the network logical entities work in collaboration, these logical entities are client and server. The essential characteristics of the model of C/S are:

- **Resource Sharing**: A server is required to provide its services to various clients at a given instance of time. For this purpose, resource sharing is an essential function performed by the server.
- **Location Transparency**: In order to mask the server location from the client, the software of the client-server performs service calls redirection when the requirement arises. This function is essential to perform as in the distributed system a server and client can be located on single machines as well as different machines.
- **Service**: On different machines, there are various processes that run which is nothing more than a relationship between client and server. Primarily the services of client and server architecture are consumed by the client. The services provided are in terms of data storage, data extraction and data transmission, etc. which the client requests from the server.
- **Asymmetrical Protocols**: The client and server have many to one relation among them in which the clients initiate the communication process. When the clients require to perform a task over the network, they invoke a request of service from the

server which is then processed by the server and required results are provided to the clients.

- **Exchanges based on Message**: The interaction among the clients and server are coupled with the help of a messaging scheme in which the service request from clients and reply from the server performs via messages.
- **Service Encapsulation**: When the server is requested to perform a task then it is solely dependent on the process by which the server will complete the task. The server has to perform various tasks at once and hence it is required to be implemented with an encapsulation mechanism that performs each task parallel without interrupting the process of the task.

6.4. ADVANTAGES AND DRAWBACKS OF CLIENT-SERVER ARCHITECTURE

6.4.1. Advantages of Client-Server Architecture

The architecture of the client-server is built in such a manner that it has the ability to provide a user interface that is cost-effective, application services, connectivity, and data storage. The organizations that are currently using this architecture do not use it to its full potential.

- **Data Sharing Enhancement:** The data sharing process in the C/S architecture is done in an enhanced manner as all the users that are authorized for data access from the server can avail the data as soon as it is available on the server. The data manipulation is performed with the help of structured query language.
- **Interoperability and Interchangeability of the Data:** SQL is a query language that is used for defining data over the network. The business organizations that use distributed database services provide access to the data to various employees. Thus, there is an issue that occurs in this case which is original data manipulation.

Hence, in order to deal with this issue, there are copies of data saved over the database and the users manipulate their version of data and save it for future use. In this manner, the interchangeability of data does not cause any issue for the organization.

- **Data and Processing are Independent of Location:** With the help of distributed client-server architecture, the user does not have to worry about the location of service request processing. The user does not consider various factors that might involve in the process of request processing. User is not supposed to get the information related to the location of processing of its service request, they only require the response of their query from the server.

Previously, while performing operations over the database there were various functionalities that were visible to the user such as the method of navigation, error messages, function keys and security. These processes are not very important for the user as they only care about the end result.

6.4.2. Drawbacks of Client-Server Architecture

Traffic congestion is one of the major issues of this architecture, due to the fact that whenever the number of requests from clients increases the server overloading issue arises. This causes the server to freeze and, in many cases, the server does not show any results and may be subjected to malfunction.

When compared to the peer to peer network, this is a major issue of this architecture. In peer to peer network, the addition of nodes increases the bandwidth of the network. One of the major drawbacks of this architecture is that in case a server fails then the service requests of the client are not fulfilled.

While in a peer to peer network the resources are available at different nodes so when the client requests service for data from one node and that node is not available then another node will perform that task. This reduces the time delay for a service request to process and the client gets the desired result.

Also, the users are required to be properly trained about working on the client/server architecture and they should be made aware of the security vulnerabilities as well. This will reduce the chances of any mishappening from the client that makes the hackers access the server files via client machines.

6.5. CLIENT-SERVER ARCHITECTURE TYPES

The client-server architecture is of three different types that are 1 tier, 2 tier and 3 tier architecture and all three have different functionalities, features, and use. The type of architecture required to be implemented is based on the requirements that the user has.

This is the benefit of distributed database architecture that helps to cater to the business of all kinds of data storage needs. This section evaluates all the three architectures of the client-server and the essential information related to them are provided.

6.5.1. One-Tier Architecture

It is evident from the name of the architecture that includes every component of the application at a single platform. The elements of the architecture that are middleware, data present at the back end and interface in one place.

The drawback of such an architecture is that it has various complexity in managing the data and the server can act inappropriately if subjected to a large number of requests at once. The examples of 1-Tier architecture are MS Office and MP3 Player.

This type of architecture has limited security issues but has major issues related to the handling of a large number of client requests. Thus, it is generally used for simple applications that do not have a large number of users active at once over the network.

6.5.2. Two-Tier Architecture

This is an advanced version of One-Tier architecture in which there are separate platforms for both user interface and servers. The client machine has the user interface from where the user requests the services from the server and the server contains the database.

Ahmed in the year 2017 reviewed that the server receives the request and responds accordingly as per the requirements. The maintenance of the business and database logic is very essential; however, both of these can be present at the server or client. There are two types of architecture present in the Two-Tier system namely fat client thin server and thin client fat server.

The difference between these two architectures is that in case of a fat client thin server both types of logics that are business and data are present at client node and in case of thin client fat server these logics are taken care of at the server node.

6.5.3. Three-Tier Architecture

This is a much secured and most recommended architecture due to the amount of security it provides. The security provided to the system is in terms of implementing an extra layer between client and server. The extra layer that has been implemented is a middleware that gets the service request from the client and provides the proper response from the server to the client.

With the help of middleware, the flexibility of the system increases and also the performance also elevates. There are three major parts of this three-tier architecture that are database, presentation, and application layer.

All these layers are taken care of by the different areas assigned that is the presentation layer is managed by the client system, the application layer is maintained by the application server and the database layer is maintained by the server system.

Although, the three-tier architecture is expensive and complex still it is required for the efficient working of the online businesses. The productivity is increased with the help of user interfaces that are cost-efficient and also helps the businesses to provide better services to its users.

The three layers involved can be evaluated as data, business, and presentation layer. The involvement of all these layers makes the working of a three-tier architecture effective (Figure 6.2).

- **Presentation Layer:** This layer is present at the top of the application which deals with the clients when a client accesses a software, they are subjected to the presentation layer. The clients send service requests to the server which is collected at the presentation layer. So, it can be said that it works as an interface to the client where it generates its query for the service.
- **Business Layer:** It is considered as the logical layer, where the service request generated by the client is sent to. This layer then further processes the service request and as per the query data is sent from the server to the clients. All the communication processes among databases and presentations are performed via the business layer.

Here, the client computer sends the service to the application layer which further processes it tops the database layer. The database layer processes the service request and sends the required data to the application layer which then further sends it to the client layer.

- **Data Layer:** This layer stores the data; the business layer connects with the database layer for data retrieval. The actions such as deletion, insertion, and updating are performed at this layer.

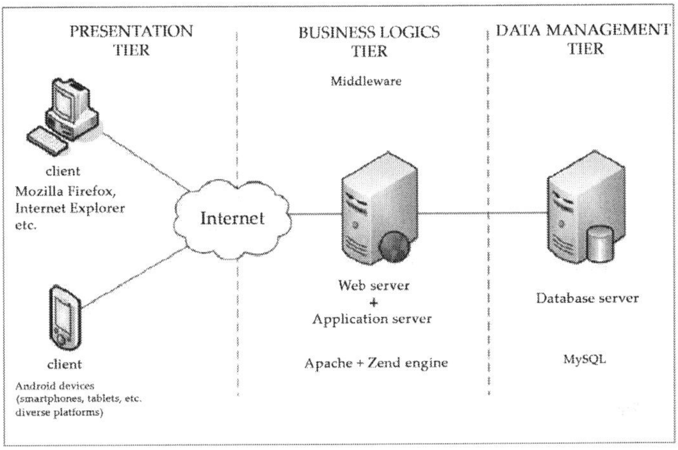

Figure 6.2: Three tier client-server architecture.

Source: Image by ResearchGate.

6.6. CONCEPT OF MIDDLEWARE IN CLIENT-SERVER MODEL

The working of both distributed and centralized systems are different as in the case of a centralized system more than one client node communicates to a central server. The centralized system is being used by various organizations that process the client request using a single centralized server.

The distributed system applies a different approach than a centralized system, in case of the distributed system a client request is processed using different nodes that behave as a server node. The results are gathered by these nodes and are provided to the client node.

The major layer that the client-server model has, specifically, the three-tier architecture, is that it contains a middleware that serves the purpose of receiving a request from the client and transmit results to the client from servers. There is an increased layer of security that this layer has in terms of user data security. The positioning is in such a manner that it is present in between the application and operating system.

6.6.1. Tasks Performed by Middleware

There are a variety of tasks available that the middleware performs, here, only the applications based on objects are considered as it has the similar functionality of a distributed system. Thus, reflecting on the functionality of an object model different tasks performed by the middleware can be assessed.

One of the major influences that the middleware has over the working of a client-server architecture is that the client nodes present over the network have varied functionalities and specifications such as operating system, processing power, etc.

Middleware also reduces the visibility of the distributed nature of a client-server architecture. The server is a combination of various nodes present over the network. When the requirement arises various nodes over the network acts as the server and provides the result to the client query.

Middleware provides a unified environment where all the nodes work similarly irrespective of their operating system, the protocol of communication and hardware specifications, etc. A common framework is provided by the middleware that enables the efficient working of the C/S environment.

6.6.2. Middleware Uses

Till now the major working of the middleware is described and the various factors related to the abstraction and process hiding that it performs have been described. Here the different uses of middleware will be discussed. Different middleware uses are:

- **Managing Transactions:** Individual transactions such as service request and service processing are managed by the middleware so it can be analyzed that no such process that might harm the system has entered.
- **Directory System:** The middleware often works as a directory system for the client programs that enables service allocation in a distributed system.
- **Security:** The major function of security that middleware performs is that it implements the authentication process. This process enables the identification of the user and then authorize them to use the database services. It helps in user data security by

reducing the chances of DoS attack, it is prevented by securing the network by implementing user authentication majors.

6.6.3. Middleware Types

In simple terms, a middleware is a process that is implemented between the database and client program. Based on their functionality the middleware is of different types such as:

- **Message Oriented Middleware:** This type of middleware allows data transmission among the applications in the form of self-contained message units that uses a communication channel. The environment provided by the MOM is the type of communication environment in which messages are transmitted asynchronously (Chappell, 2018).
- **RPC Middleware:** RPC stands for Remote Procedure Call which is a type of middleware that allows a program present over a local system to request a service from a remote server. The RPC allows this process to work in an efficient manner without the local system requiring any details of the network.
- **Object Middleware**: This is a type of middleware that allows different objects of distributing the environment for the communication control process. The essential functionality of this middleware is that it allows program calls among different nodes present over a distributed network.
- **Database Middleware:** The client and server nodes present over a distributed network have permission to interact with the database directly in this type of middleware. An example of a database middleware is the SQL database.

6.7. THIN CLIENT/SERVER MODEL

A thin client in the client-server model is referred to as the user computing node that is heavily dependent on the server for all the computations. These clients have very low processing power and hardware specifications that make them dependent on the server's capabilities and they do not do much by themselves.

Although each node in a distributed environment can behave like a server the term 'thin client' makes it clear that not every device has the specifications to be the server. The advantage of using thin clients is that for malware attacks they are less vulnerable, their life cycle is longer, they have less power consumption, and also these are cheap and easily available.

Kanter in the year 2000 reviewed and stated that the communication protocols used by the thin client are Remote desktop protocol (RDP) and Independent Architecture of Computing (ICA). There is also one more protocol named X that is used by the devices connected locally and this protocol not useful for remote computing (Figure 6.3).

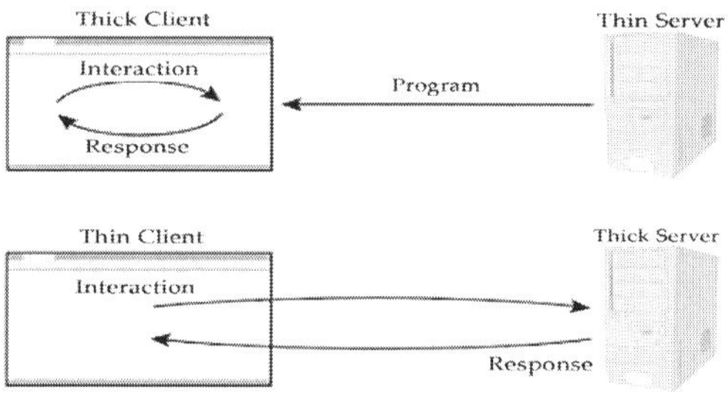

Figure 6.3: Thin client-server architecture.

Source: Image by Wikimedia.

The benefits of using a thin client system are in terms of cost savings. There are different aspects of *cost savings* provided by the thin client system such as cost of IT support, cost of purchase, licensing, and capital cost, it decreases data center cost by using minimum space and the operating and administration cost are reduced up to 70%. There is a huge saving in energy cost as using thin client architecture reduces the cost of energy by up to 90% which helps in carbon foot printing reduction.

The management of thin clients is very simple as the data center is responsible for upgrading hardware and software, changes in application and security procedures. The requirement of the IT department is reduced and the downtime is also less and it simplifies the backups of data with the help of a centralized system.

In terms of security, the thin clients are not subjected to unauthorized and harmful software, data is saved only at the server and there is no other location where the data is being stored. The monitoring and management of the system are easier due to the use of a centralized system of processing.

6.8. THICK CLIENT/SERVER MODEL

The thick client-server architecture has the client node efficient enough to carry out its own functionalities. In comparison with the thin client model, the thick client architecture has all the specifications to perform functionalities on their own. The software and hardware requirements required to perform complex functionalities are available at the client nodes.

Some of the essential factors required to be considered for thick client-server architecture are that it is an expensive deployment process, the client performs data verification, communication with the server is not required at regular intervals, the resource requirement is high and the only few servers are required. The major drawback is that it has a high-security threat than the thin client-server model.

The thick clients are implemented over the network when the server requirements are lower. Thick clients are not made available to the employees of an Organization, due to the threat of local files misuse. The advantage of using thick clients over thin ones is that due to the availability of own resources the thick client performs the majority of functionality and it is not much dependent on the server. Apart from data transmission, the thick client does not communicate with the server (Figure 6.4).

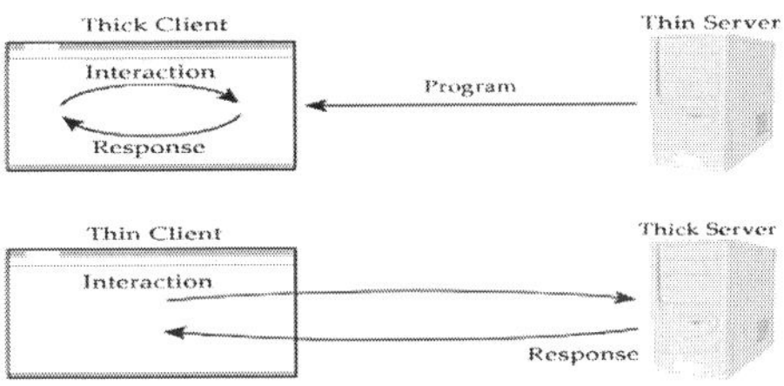

Figure 6.4: Thick client-server architecture.

Source: Image by Wikimedia.

The benefits of using thick clients are that the graphic user interface is rich that allows graphical intensiveness to be provided to the clients. The programming processes that require a huge amount of resources are provided by the thick clients as they have the resource to perform such activities.

Thick clients also do not have to be dependent on the server's processing as the local machines in itself are efficient to perform high processing tasks. This increases the server capacity and allows it to serve an increased number of clients. One more advantage of using such a client is that it can perform tasks offline and only required to be connected to the server in case of data synchronization.

6.9. SERVICES OF CLIENT-SIDE IN C/S ARCHITECTURE

There are a variety of services that a client node performs in a client-server architecture as it communicates with the server for every query that is being asked for it to perform. This section will describe the services that the client node performs in a client-server architecture.

The services of client-side include:

- Application and network services;
- Database services;
- Dynamic data exchange;
- Message services;
- Object linking and embedding (OLE);
- Print services;
- Remote services; and
- Utility services.

Remote services that the client-side performs include processes such as backup services and host data downloads, etc. These services are very beneficial for the businesses that have their clients at remote places, hence, using the remote services they manage these activities. The major services of the client-side can be considered as dynamic data exchangeand OLE.

DDE protocol or the dynamic data exchange is an effective technique that allows performing data transmission seamlessly at every platform. Shared memory is used to exchange data among different applications. There is a message set present in the DDE protocol for communication purposes.

The OLE protocol further helps the users in data encompassing different file formats so that data manipulation software is not required by the users. The process of object linking allows the client node to link different data in a single object so that not much processing is required at the client-side. In order to use the OLE services, there is a dedicated SDK that allows working at all platforms that might not support the OLE techniques.

6.10. SERVICES OF SERVER-SIDE IN C/S ARCHITECTURE

6.10.1. Processing of Request

The server has essential functions in a C/S architecture and is required to perform various services, in which the major service is request processing. Here the majority of services performed by the client-side are described by considering various factors associated with it.

Request processing is an essential service performed by the server-side. In order to process the request by the client, the server follows some steps in a systematic manner. At first, the network operating system software of service that is present at the client machine gets issued by the service from the client.

The requests are formatted appropriately by these services into a remote procedure call which is then issued to the layer of application present at the stack of client protocol. Now, this request is received by the server via a layer of application of the server's stack of the protocol.

6.10.2. Print Services

The shared server supports natural processes such as plotters, faxes, and printers. The server is required to accept various inputs at once. Based on the priority of the task the requests are queued at the server and then they are handled as per device availability. This process allows cost saving for the business on a large scale because the allocated works are queued and are only performed when the cost of the communication is lower.

6.10.3. File Services

The distributed computing environment (DCE) provided the system of distributed files. This type of service has some benefits such as data sharing among clients is performed with ease, centralized administration is provided and server security is provided for securing all data. A physical file system has fewer components than a C/S architecture of the simplest form. It includes a file system at the client-side and server-side.

In order to retrieve data from the server the client application has to perform system call, this system call is issued to the file system at the client-side. The file system at the client-side then gets the desired data from the file system of the server-side which is then sent to the client application via the client-side. This process of file access is transparent in nature as the client application does not has any API for the file access.

6.10.4. Security Services

The security of the client and server in a C/S architecture is a very essential process. The implementation of effective security protocol helps increase the user trust for the services as they are assured that their data will not get leaked or stolen due to insecure communication or data transmission process. The security services provided on the server-side of the C/S architecture depends on various factors.

The host environment provides some effective security services which are required to be provided by the C/S applications. The major and most effective security technique is user authentication in which the user is provided with a login ID and password so that the user can access database services securely.

There are some data encryption methods also present which are used to enhance the security services. The data present in an encrypted form is not easily decrypted. There are various combinations that the intruder or attacker has to perform in order to decrypt the data and that process takes a lot of time.

6.10.5. Services by Database

The database services range to various activities that particularly deals with data storage and data extraction. When the requests are received by the server then the server performs the process of locking and checking the request. A lock table is created by the database which is invoked in case a lock check is created.

The access for the record is given to record level so the primary key is considered for providing appropriate records to the client. There is an issue in this system as it lacks the procedural code execution, which increases the factor of record locking. In this case, if the number of client request increase that causes malfunctioning in the behavior of database services.

The data management techniques use file services so that efficient space allocation can be done. The use of structured query language (SQL) helps in data extraction directly from the space where they are kept. The SQL queries invoke rows and tables where the desired data is present.

In order to work in an efficient manner, there are some features that the distributed database is required to have such as:

- The ability of database splitting among disk drivers;
- Back out of the dynamic transaction process;
- Data integrity by locking mechanism;
- Detection of deadlock;
- Features for managing remote distributed DB;
- Form of rollback;
- Mirrored database support (for file recovery);
- Prevention of deadlock;
- Processing of multithreaded application;
- Reclamation of files;
- Recovery and detection of error should be automatic;
- Recovery of the audit file; and
- Tools for performance optimization.

6.11. REMOTE PROCEDURE CALL

RPC is a technique used in a distributed system like the client-server model, where the access of data and information is required to be performed remotely. When the procedure that is saved on a machine is located at a remote location, then the RPC is required to be used. It allows the communication process to be remotely conducted via procedure calls.

This is performed when the local client requires access to a file present in a machine stored at a remote location. So, for that, the local machine invokes a procedure call to its own application layer which is then processed to the application layer of the remote server. The remote server application sends this call to the database which then replies with the required file and the file is then sent to the client following a similar process.

Now, in order to perform this process, the major requirement is that calling and called both the procedures should have the same address space. RPC allows the programmers to hide the interface details from the network. The programming of the client-server model becomes easier with the help of RPC and also makes more power. The major components involved in the architecture of RPC are client, server, RPC runtime, and client and server stub.

6.11.1. Issues of Remote Procedure Call

The major RPC issues are Marshalling, semantics, binding, transport protocol and exception handling. There is also an issue related to the transparency in the RPC, as the local procedure call should be replaced with client and server stubs at their respective ends. But it cannot be achieved, due to a number of factors that are described as:

- **Service Numbering:** While specifying the RPC interfacing it is the programmer's responsibility that every service has a service number assigned to it. This is extremely important that any other service does not have the same number that has already been assigned to another service. The system is required to check whether the numbers assigned are unique to every service or not.

In case it is not unique then there will be some major issues with the working of the RPC in a client-server architecture. The issues will be in the form that two services that have been assigned the same number will not provide desired results to the user.

- **Transport Protocol:** The libraries that are supported by the RPC are TCP and UDP but it has been theorized that any transport protocol can be replaced by Sun RPC but it is not practically possible. The protocol selection is the responsibility of the programmer and that selection decides how to call semantics can be affected. A broadcast procedure call is supported by the RPC which allows all the servers present on the network to reply.
- **Parameter Passing:** The parameter passing approach of the call by value is supported by the RPC in which one parameter is passed that provides a single result. However, there are various data items can be present in a single parameter. The global variables cannot be accessed by RPC because it is performed between a client and a server.

6.11.2. Failure Handling

The analysis of RPC showed that there are majorly five failure classes that have higher chances of occurrence in the system of RPC. These are server location is disabled for clients, request message is lost which is sent from client to the server for a service, reply message is lost which is sent from server to client, upon receiving request the server becomes unable to respond or crashes and it also may happen that after the request is sent by the client it gets crashed.

6.12. SECURITY OF CLIENT-SERVER ARCHITECTURE

The popularity of the C/S architecture is majorly due to the service processing separation which increases the efficiency of the architecture based on cost, maximum use of resources and decreased traffic over the network. However, there is a drawback of this feature which has been identified to be a major vulnerability to security.

The service distribution among clients and servers increases the issue of a security breach leading them to misuse and damage of property. The areas required to be considered for security include all the factors associated with client/server system (C/S system). These include local and wide area networks (WANs), the client system and hosts. The security protocols are, however, implemented but they do not have their impact immediately.

According to John McAfee "When a hacker gains access to any corporate data, the value of that data depends on which server, or sometimes a single person's computer, that the hacker gains access to."

The major areas of security that require focus are user and client security, network, and server security, and security of firewalls and endpoint. These factors are discussed in this section efficiently considering all the above-mentioned security aspects.

6.12.1. User and Client Security

The system which is a very essential part of a client-server system and at the same time most vulnerable to security breaches is the client system. The client systems are mostly desktops that work with minimal security processes. Clients request service from a server and for that, they establish a connection to the server which is in most cases of a security breach are unsecured or were open for access.

This open connection or unsecured connection becomes a major cause of security breach as the hackers use it as an entry point to the servers. Although, there is some form of security present at the client level such as locks for disk drive so that any malicious software gets prohibited from entering the system but still there is a gap in security, that is present in the form of accessibility for the data present on client's system.

One of the very basic issues of security occurs in case the user has set a password which can be guessed easily or they even share the password of their system which may result in unauthorized access. This happens because the system can only identify whether the user is authorized or not is by the user authentication process and whoever has access to it is considered to be the authorized user.

Hence, it can be assumed that users are the main culprits of the security breach as the first and foremost security defense is authentication and identification of the user. Thus, it becomes very prominent to use advanced passwords and the user should be aware of the security risks of the authentication process. Apart from these the organizations should implement some essential rules for user authentication and only the trusted employees should be allowed to have the authentication information.

6.12.2. Network and Server Security

Software protection is not the only security paradigm that is required to be considered instead it should be implemented at every level to create a more secure environment. The environment in which the servers are located should be access controlled. The administration provided to the server needs to be given to the authorized person. Database server access control is the main aspect of server security.

Database access should be complying with the policy of password set by considering the standards of a business set previously. There are various ways in which the data protection protocol for user data security can be considered. One of the most reliable data protection technique is to use the encryption technique. The data encryption allows the data to be stored in an encrypted form which can only be decrypted with proper information that uses a mechanism of DES.

Other security-related aspects are that the location of the web server and database backend must be different. Also, in case of a brute force attack and trial and error attack, the delay in response should be provided to the user. There are some other risks also identified for the model of client-server such as model development risk of client-server architecture, risks related to the workstation, risk of network wire, and the risk of a database of management.

The networks are vulnerable to security attacks such as unauthorized eavesdropping, DoS attack and data packets modification. The unauthorized eavesdropping process is performed by the hackers in which they monitor the data over the network and can steal information that is very sensitive to the user. In case the user is a business organization then it will be a topic of great concern for the company.

In a DoS attack, computer systems are made unavailable to respond to a query. Web servers are the major target of this type of attack. The major attacks involved in the DoS are service and message overloading. The service overloading will attack the server in which any additional service request will not process.

The DoS attack is also caused via message overloading in which the attacker sends files of large sizes to the server at regular intervals. This causes the message box of the server to get fully occupied that increases the service requests and at the end disk crash is caused. The modification of packet attack is of growing concern, in this attack the hacker modifies the information of the data packet.

This process takes place when the client sends a service request which is sent to the server in form of a data packet now, the attacker if gets the authentication for the data packet then he will change the contents of the data packet and the client will get the information other than desired. In many cases, the attacker even destroys the contents of the packet.

6.12.3. Firewall and End-Point Security

The security strategies for client-server architecture includes endpoint security in which firewall security is considered. The program of endpoint security includes a security software that is installed on every device located over a network. The host of the security program is the gateway or server where the security is centralized.

A firewall program is a simple form of endpoint security, this firewall is installed over a single desktop for protecting user data which is transferred via the internet. The connections to the server via user machine are in most cases remain open and IP address that is static is used so it provides the hackers ease to enter into a network. The firewalls are installed among the transaction layer and user machine, the connections among physical machines are implemented with internet protocols' (IPs) lowest level.

The service request from clients is translated to packets by firewalls, the address is provided by incoming packets decoding and at last, it decodes the channel. Thus, internet connections are controlled by the firewalls as they act among the transaction layer and user machine. They are also responsible for filtering network traffic that is inbound and outbound, and if they find any activity that is suspicious then it makes the user aware of it.

6.12.4. Encryption Algorithms

6.12.4.1. Symmetric Encryption

This type of encryption is also known as secret-key cryptography, where encryption and decryption of data are performed with the help of similar keys and algorithms. This type of encryption has the vulnerability that both data and the key have the same security due to their storage. Also, the hacker can get access to encrypted data and read it without much hustle.

The advantage of such a system is that both the data and the key are not required to be secured only the security of the key is required. In case open communication channels are used then the encryption will no longer remain effective as both the key and data will be sent over one channel and everyone over the channel will get the data along with the key. In case the channel is itself enough secure that the key can be passed so the data can also be transferred and the key will not be required. This issue is resolved by using algorithms of key exchange (Figure 6.5).

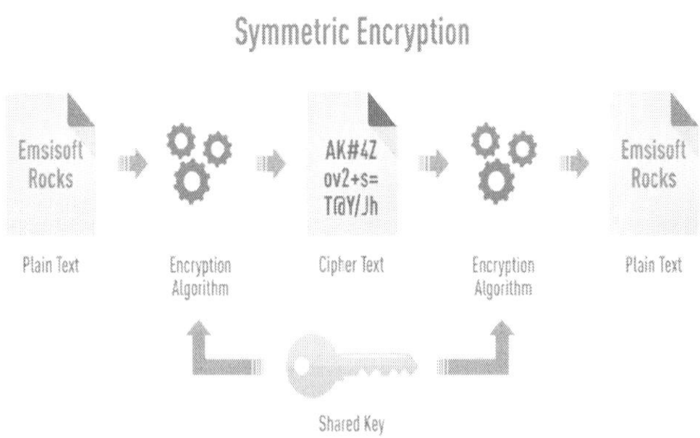

Figure 6.5: Symmetric encryption.

Source: Image by Wikimedia.

6.12.4.2. Key Creation

The process of key creation is that of generating keys that use a random number generator. The process of key generation is only reliable when it generates a unique key. The more unique the key is lesser will be the chances of the key being guessed. This criterion of key generation makes it very reliable if proper techniques are used for generating keys.

6.12.4.3. Random Number Generators

Special devices are used for generating random numbers, these generators collect data that is present in unrehearsed form like electric current fluctuation, atmospheric conditions, radioactive decay parameters, etc. Using different approaches to generating random numbers decreases its chances of being tracked by the hackers and if the numbers are generated based on similar criteria then it will be easily traced.

6.12.4.4. Block Encryption

The data required to be encrypted is divided into various blocks and every block is then encrypted using the same key. In this process, every block encrypts a large number of bits rather than bit by bit. This method is very effective as identical blocks are encrypted differently to one another. The process of block encryption, as the name suggests, encrypts every block of data that enhances the security of the data being transmitted.

6.12.4.5. Stream Encryption

This is different from block encryption; every byte is separately encrypted here. On the basis of the key, the generation of pseudo-random numbers takes place. The byte encryption is a crucial process to be followed that determines the effectiveness of the encryption technique.

It is very essential to consider how the previous byte was encrypted as on that basis the next bytes are encrypted. The productivity is very high and while using the communication channels for data transmission this information of encryption is used.

6.12.4.6. Attacking Encrypted Information

For the purpose of decrypting the encrypted data, there are two processes available such as identify the vulnerability of the algorithm or find the key. One of the most basic forms of attack performed for decryption is to use all the keys that are available. This is known as brute-force attack which provides the key for decryption but it has a drawback that it takes time. In order to get key information about that is 128-bit long estimated time might reach millions of years.

The other method of attacking encrypted data is to identify the shortcomings of the algorithm used. These shortcomings are in terms of similar behavior of data encryption and the similar pattern of data transmission which has been used. These regularities can be identified by the attacker and on the basis of that, they can predict what the next encryption will be used. This allows them to decrypt the data in a lesser amount of time which is a great cause of concern for the user.

6.13. CONCLUSION

The client-server is considered to be the most effective and most popular architecture of distributed database architecture. It consists of various benefits and drawbacks as well. The benefits allow it to be used very extensively and most of the businesses prefer a client-server architecture for their business.

It is beneficial for the business in terms of cost and energy reduction that allows them to save money as well as reduce their carbon footprint that has become an important environmental aspect. The drawbacks are present in every computing system and using security procedures these drawbacks can be mitigated.

The middleware provides the services to be performed in a systematic and more secure manner, it differentiates between client and server and also provides hiding to the processes that are not important to be visible to the clients. The unified environment is provided by the middleware where irrespective of the computing specifications the clients are allowed to perform their tasks.

There are two types of models are present in client-server architecture namely, thin client and thick client, both of these are essential to serving clients with different needs. This chapter efficiently describes the efficiency and drawbacks of both these models and where each of them can be used. Also, there are different services performed by the clients and servers in a client-server architecture.

The remote procedure call is of utmost importance in a client-server architecture because either the client or the server can be located in a remote location and in order to perform the task, they are required to be communicating with each other. They do so with the help of a remote procedure call that allows the clients and servers to connect with each other even if they are located remotely.

Security aspects of the client-server architecture are essential as the architecture is vulnerable to cyber-attacks. The four major aspects that have been discussed in this chapter in terms of security are user and client security, network, and server security, firewall, and end-point security and encryption algorithms. Majorly the clients are responsible for any type of attack over the server due to their lack of attention towards the security of their system.

This chapter analyses the aspects of all the major factors associated with client and server architecture and more focus is given to the security paradigm. The services provided by this architecture make it very popular among its users and the process of splitting the services makes it more secure and increases the requesting and replying to the services by clients and servers.

REFERENCES

1. Ahmed, F., (2017). *Concepts of Database Architecture*. [online] Medium. Available at: https://medium.com/oceanize-geeks/concepts-of-database-architecture-dfdc558a93e4 (accessed on 1 June 2020).
2. Apachebooster, (2018). *What is Client-Server Architecture and What are its Types?* [online] Available at: https://apachebooster.com/blog/what-is-client-server-architecture-and-what-are-its-types/ (accessed on 1 June 2020).
3. Caballé, S., Xhafa, F., Raya, J., Uchida, K., & Barolli, L., (2014). *Building a Software Service for Mobile Devices to Enhance Awareness in Web Collaboration*. [ebook] Available at: https://www.researchgate.net/figure/3-tier-architecture_fig1_277187696 (accessed on 1 June 2020).
4. Chappell, D., (2018). *Enterprise Service Bus*. [online] O'Reilly Online Learning. Available at: https://www.oreilly.com/library/view/enterprise-service-bus/0596006756/ch05.html (accessed on 1 June 2020).
5. Commons.wikimedia.org. (2014). *File: DotNet Remoting Architecture.png - Wikimedia Commons*. [online] Available at: https://commons.wikimedia.org/wiki/File:DotNet_Remoting_Architecture.png (accessed on 1 June 2020).
6. Exforsys.com. (2007). *Client-Server Security | IT Training and Consulting-Exforsys*. [online] Available at: http://www.exforsys.com/tutorials/client-server/client-server-security.html (accessed on 1 June 2020).
7. Ganbold, M., (2017). *File: Symmetric Encryption.png -Wikimedia Commons*. [online] Commons.wikimedia.org. Available at: https://commons.wikimedia.org/wiki/File:Symmetric_encryption.png (accessed on 1 June 2020).
8. Guru99.com. (2020). *DBMS Architecture: 1-Tier, 2-Tier & 3-Tier*. [online] Available at: https://www.guru99.com/dbms-architecture.html (accessed on 1 June 2020).
9. Kanter, J., (2000). [ebook] Pdfs.semanticscholar.org. Available at: https://pdfs.semanticscholar.org/2e4c/9056a48b46ba3b2e8af28fe429c26aac3f5d.pdf (accessed on 1 June 2020).
10. Sack, C., (2012). *File: Thin Client-Thick Client.jpg-Wikimedia Commons*. [online] Commons.wikimedia.org. Available at: https://

commons.wikimedia.org/wiki/File:Thin_Client-Thick_Client.jpg (accessed on 1 June 2020).

11. Saintangelos.com. (2020). *Client Server Architecture*. [online] Available at: http://saintangelos.com/studentdesk/Download/CLIENT%20 SERVER%20ARCHITECTURE.PDF (accessed on 1 June 2020).
12. Secure Blackbox. (2020). *Securing Your Client-Server or Multi-Tier Application*. [online] Available at: https://www.secureblackbox.com/kb/articles/Securing-client-server-app.rst (accessed on 1 June 2020).

CHAPTER 7

Database Management System: A Practical Approach

CONTENTS

7.1. Introduction 176

7.2. Components of a Database 178

7.3. Database Management System 179

7.4. The Relational Model 188

7.5. Functional Dependency and Normalization 189

7.6. De Normalization 189

7.7. Structured Query Language (SQL) 191

7.8. Query by Example (QBE) 194

7.9. Database Recovery System 195

7.10. Query Processing 196

7.11. Query Optimization 197

7.12. Database Tuning 199

7.13. Data Migration 199

7.14. Conclusion 200

References 201

The database is a computerized software to store data of the individual user or the business organization. The data stored in a database are inter-related to each other so that different processes like deletion, insertion, retrieval, and modification of data can be performed in an efficient manner.

The data in a database is stored in various forms such as reports, schemas, views, and tables. There is computer software available to manage the database and this software is called a database management system.

The functions such as storage and data retrieval are performed under required security measures in a database management system. The database manipulation is performed with the help of various programs. In order to retrieve data from the database users provide queries to the database system. This query is then processed by the DBMS and proper result is retrieved and provided to the user.

At first, the evaluates the database system and its components. Then various functions related to the working of DBMS are described. At last, more functions of the database management systems such as database tuning and data migration are evaluated. The query processing is described in detail as it is the most essential process to be performed in a DBMS.

7.1. INTRODUCTION

In the present business, world data is of utmost importance for the business organizations and for the users of the online services data is a major attribute that they do not want to lose. Business organizations use database services to store the data of their users and for different business operations performed within a business.

The database is a system that stores information in a structured form. There is a huge collection of information is provided by every user and that immense amount of data needs to be stored by the organization.

Business organizations collect a huge amount of data every day, this data is required to be collected and stored in a secured manner. Data is considered to be an essential resource for the organization and the companies have a competitive edge over their rivals if they manage their data efficiently.

The data needs to be stored in an accurate and reliable manner so that the decision-making process for the business becomes more efficient. It is not an easy job to provide people with essential data that they require at the right time due to the availability of a huge amount of data.

The data management is an essential process for every business organization and if they are able to manage this data efficiently than they can achieve more success in business. Hence, database management has become a priority for every business organization.

A database system allows data management with much more simplification and also provides information extraction in a timely manner. The database system allows the collection of related files and also allows data interpretation. A database management system (DBMS) is a type of software that has the ability for data access.

The DBMS has the objective of providing the users and business organization to retrieve, store, and define the information that is stored in a database. A database and system of database management are a very important part of various organizations such as banks, universities, schools, government, and business organizations.

For any business, organization data is a basic and essential resource. In order to have an essential organizational working the management and organization of data are important. Data collected by the business organizations are in different forms such as text, images, videos, documents, etc.

Data are the raw information that provides relevant information after the analysis. There is a single difference between data and information which is that the information is collected after data refinement.

In the current scenario, there is a huge amount of data present but the quality information is very less. With quality information, it means that information is relevant, timely, and accurate that is considered to be the main attribute of information.

The three major attributes associated with information are accuracy, timeliness, and relevancy. Accurate data is free from all types of errors and provides the meaning of data accurately. Accurate data also has the functionality of non-biasness that it should not have any type of opinion related to it and should show the result of what the data is representing.

The timelines attribute of data represents that the data is provided to the user at the time of requirement. In the current scenario, if a system is less time consuming then it has a higher chance of succeeding in the market. This attribute is present in a database system.

Relevancy is the attribute of information that shows that the provided data is relevant to what the user is required to have. This attribute is subjective

various functions such as insertion of data, deletion, and updating of data are performed.

Thus, it becomes very essential to manage all the functions that are performed in a database and their management is required. A DBMS is a type of interface provided for the users between stored data and application programs.

The DBMS can also be defined as a system that performs computerized record-keeping in which the users are allowed to perform actions related to changing the data such as updating the data, retrieve, modify, and delete the data that is not required.

There are some primary functions that a DBMS system performs such as database organization. create and define the database. As there are various data elements present in a database, sop to access this data it is very essential to connect the data elements as per some form of relationship among them. This relation among the data elements allows the data to be retrieved in less time and with more efficiency (Figure 7.1).

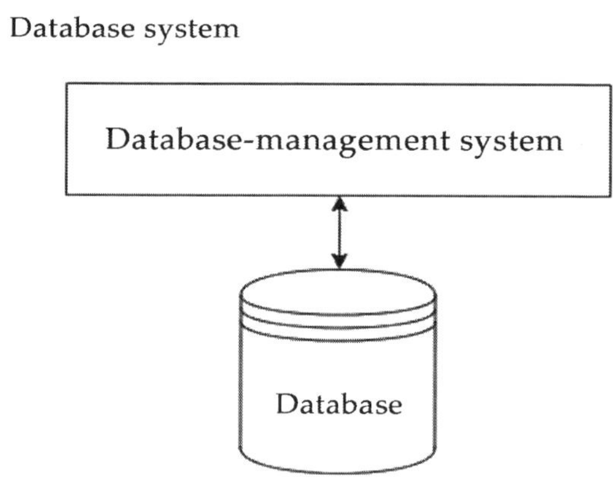

Figure 7.1: Database management system.

Source: Image by Gitlab.

For relationship development among the data elements schemas and subschema's are developed among the data. A DBMS system performs tasks such as input data by which the user is allowed to enter the data that they wanted to store in a database.

Data processing is the process by which data manipulation is performed in a DBMS. The data stored in the database can be altercated by the user if the data is wrongly entered or there are some changes in the data is found.

Another essential factor for a DBMS is that it is required to maintain the integrity of data and its security. The security is provided for the user's data with the help of authorization by which the users are provided with login access and are not allowed to share this information with someone else. This process is helpful in data integrity and the security of data.

7.3.1. Components of DBMS

There are three major components of a DBMS such as structured query language (SQL), data manipulation language (DML), and data definition language.

- **Data Definition Language (DDL):** The structure of database objects is created and modified in a database with the help of DDL. The objects in a database include indexes, tables, schemas, and views. Also, as the name suggests DDL is used to define the data elements and records that are being stored in a database system.
- **Data Manipulation Language (DML):** DML is a syntax element set for managing the data. These syntaxes allow the user to make changes to already present data in the database. Every type of data manipulation that is being governed in a database are performed with the help of this language.
- **Structured Query Language (SQL):** SQL is a query language used in a database where database systems are commanded by the user for the addition of data, deletion, and modification of data with the help of some queries. Its application is of major focus in the relational database for the purpose of management and retrieval of data.

It is used in the relational database because in a relational database the data is stored in a structured form and thus SQL is used to perform actions like create and maintain databases. Data stored in a structured manner allows the database to perform the actions easily and the time taken to perform these functions are also less (Figure 7.2).

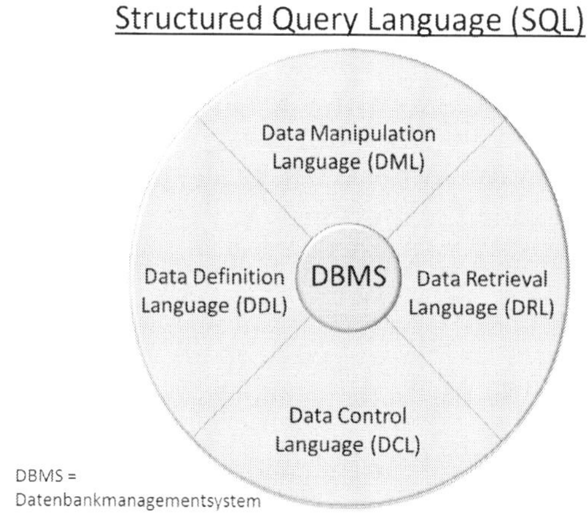

Figure 7.2:SQL for database.

Source: Image by Wikimedia.

7.3.2. Traditional File System v/s Database Systems

Conventionally, the data were stored and processed with the help of traditional file processing systems. In most of these traditional file systems, each file is independent stored irrespective of other file, and data located in diverse files can be combined only by writing individual program for each application. The data and the application programs that uses the data are arranged in such a manner that any variation related to the data entails modifying all the programs that uses the data. It is primarily because of the fact that each file is hard-coded with specific information such as size of data and type of data, etc. in some cases, it is not possible to find all the programs with that data and is recognized on a trial-and-error basis. All functional areas in the organization forms, evaluate, and distributes its own files. The files such as payroll and inventory produce separate files and have no communication with each of them.

7.3.3. Limitations of Traditional File System

- **Data Redundancy:** As it is generally seen that most of the application has their own set of data files, the same type of data may be required to be recorded and stored in many files. For instance, payroll file and personal file, both contain the complete data the name of employees, and their designation, etc. The result is redundant or duplicate data items. This redundancy thus necessitates the need of additional or extra storage capacity, higher cost or time that need to be given, as well as additional efforts and hard work require in keeping all files up to-date.

- **Data Inconsistency:** Data redundancy is the major reason that cause data inconsistency particularly when data is to be updated. Data inconsistency may likely be occurred if there are large number of same data items that present in more than one file and that do not update simultaneously in each and every file. For instance, suppose an employee shift to higher position which is from Clerk to Superintendent and the same is instantly updated in the payroll file may not certainly be updated in provident fund file as well. This results in two different designations of an employee at the same time in the system. Over the period of time, such type of discrepancies may hamper the overall quality of information that is contain in the data file which impact the accuracy of reports.
- **Lack of Data Integration:** Since there is existence of independent data file, users may face difficulty in receiving information on any ad hoc query that needs accessing the data stored in many files. In such kind of scenario, complicated programs have to be developed in a way to recover data from every file or the users have to physically gather the required information.
- **Program Dependence:** It is generally seen that the reports which are created by the file processing system are program dependent, which means if any change in the structure or format of records and data in the file is to be made, the programs have to modify accordingly. Also, it is required to develop a new program to produce a new report.
- **Data Dependence:** The Applications/programs in the file processing system are data dependent which means, the physical location of file, file organization, as well as retrieval of data from the storage media are dictated by the necessities of the particular application. For example, in payroll application, the file may be prepared based on employee records that is sorted by their last name, which means accessing the data related to employee's record can be possible only by searching their last name.

- **Limited Data Sharing:** It is generally seen that there are limited data sharing possibilities with the traditional file system. Each application carries its own private files and users possess with the limited ability to share the data outside their own applications. Complex programs required to be written in order to retrieve data from several incompatible files.
- **Poor Data Control:** There was no centralized control at the data element level, which means a traditional file system is completely of decentralized nature. It is also possible that the data field may have numerous names defined by the diverse departments of an organization and rely on the file it was in. This situation may be conducive to interpreting different meaning of a data field in diverse context or identical meaning for different fields. This causes poor data control.
- **Problem of Security:** It is a major challenge to comply with the security checks and access rights in a traditional file system, since application programs are added in an adhoc manner.
- **Data Manipulation Capability is Inadequate:** It is usually seen that in the traditional file systems, there is very limited ability data manipulation primarily because of the fact that they do not provide strong interconnection between data in different files.
- **Needs Excessive Programming:** There is need of an excessive programming effort in order to develop a new application program due to very high interdependence between data and program in a file system. Each application in the system requires the effort to be put by the developers in a way to start from the scratch by designing new file formats and descriptions and then write the file access logic for each new file.

7.3.4. Advantages of Database Systems

- **Controlled Redundancy:** In a traditional file system, as each application has its own data, which causes replication of common data items in more than one file. This redundancy/duplication necessitates multiple updating for a single transaction, resulting in wastage of large amount if storage. One cannot eliminate all types of discrepancies because of technical reasons. But in a database, this kind of duplication can be cautiously controlled, that means the database system is already aware of the redundancy and it assumes the duty for propagating updates.

- **Data Consistency:** The problem of updating numerous files in traditional file system may result in problem of inaccurate data as different files may carries different information of the same data item at a given point of time. This causes contradictory or incorrect information to its users. In database systems, this existing problem of data inconsistency can be inevitably solved by controlling the redundancy.
- **Program Data Independence:** The traditional file systems are in majority of the cases data dependent, which means that the access strategies and data organization are dictated by the needs of the specific application and the application programs are developed in accordance with the same specification. However, the database systems provide an independence between the application programs and file system that allows for variations at one level of the data without affecting others. This key characteristic of database systems allows to change data without any necessary changes in the application programs that process the data.
- **Sharing of Data:** In database systems, the data is centrally controlled, which means all the authorized users possess the ability to share the data. The sharing of data does not only applicable for current applications programs but new application programs can also be developed to perform on the existing data. Furthermore, it is possible to satisfy the requirements of the new application programs without any need of creating any new file.
- **Enforcement of Standards:** In database systems, data being stored at one central place, standards can easily be imposed by the DBA. This ensures standardized data formats in order to facilitate data transfers between systems. Applicable standards might include any or all of the following—installation, departmental, industry, organizational, corporate, national or international.
- **Improved Data Integrity:** Data integrity refers to ensuring that all the data contained in the database is both consistent as well as accurate. The centralized control property makes it possible to keep an eye on the quality of data, resulting in providing data integrity. One integrity check that need to be integrated into the database is to ensure that if there is a reference to certain object, that object must exist.

- **Improved Security:** Database security means ensuring the protection of data contained in the database from unauthorized users. The DBA ensures that there is complete standard or process of data to be followed before getting access to data system, including proper authentic schemes for access to the data base management systems and additional checks before authorizing access to sensitive data. The level of security could be different in context with the various types of data and operations.
- **Data Access is Efficient:** The database system often makes use of various complicated techniques and strategies to access the stored data very efficiently.
- **Conflicting Requirements Can Be Balanced:** The DBA helps in addressing the various conflicting requirements of various users and applications by knowing the overall requirements of the organization. The DBA can help in structuring the system in a way to provide an overall service which help the organization in accomplishing its goals.
- **Improved Backup and Recovery Facility:** Through its backup and recovery subsystem, the database system allows its users to recover or retrieve any files from the system in case of any hardware or software failures. The recovery subsystem of the database system is basically concerned with ensuring that the database is restored to the state it was in before the program started executing, in case of system crash.
- **Minimal Program Maintenance:** In a traditional file system, the application programs with the description of data and the logic for retrieving the data are erected independently. Thus, changes to the access methods or data formats necessitate the need to adapt the application programs. Therefore, there is always requirement of high maintenance. These can be reduced to minimal in database systems due because of freedom that data and application programs possess.
- **Data Quality is High:** As compared to the traditional file systems, the quality of data in database systems are very high. It is possible because of the existence of processes and tools in the database system.
- **Good data Accessibility and Responsiveness:** The database systems provide report writers or query languages that allow

the users to ask ad hoc queries to get the required information immediately, without the obligation of writing application programs (as in case of file system), that access the information from the database. This is possible because of integration in database systems.

- **Concurrency Control:** The database systems are primarily designed to manage simultaneous (concurrent) access of the database by large number of its clients. They also prevent any loss of integrity or loss of information due to these concurrent accesses.
- **Economical to Scale:** It is generally seen that the operational data of an organization in database systems is stored in a central database. The application programs that work on this data can be formed with minimal cost as compared with the traditional file system. This lessens the overall costs of management and operation of the database that leads to an economical scaling.
- **Increased Programmer Productivity:** The database system is generally equipped with many standard functions that the programmer would have to write in file system. The existence of these functions allows the programmers to keep their focus on the specific functionality required by the users without worrying about the implementation details. It results in enhancing the overall productivity of the programmer and also reduces the development cost and time.

7.3.5. Disadvantages of Database Systems

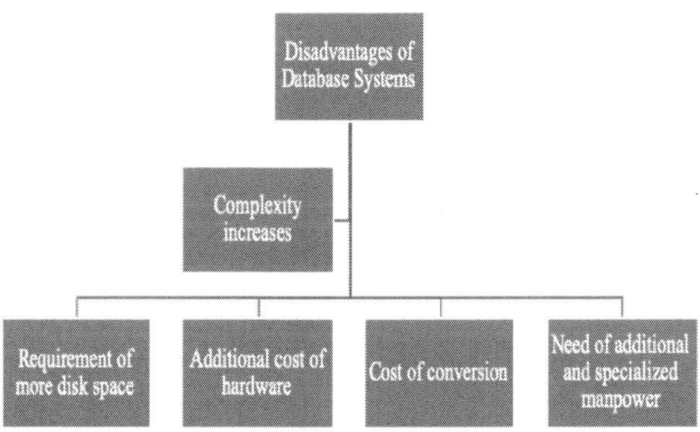

Figure 7.3: Disadvantages of data base system.

In contrast to many advantages of the database systems, DBMS also comes with various disadvantages. The disadvantages of a database system are as follows:

Complexity increases: The data structure may become more complicated due to the functioning of centralized database that support many applications in an organization. It may result in causing difficulties in its management and may require professional's expertise for management.

Requirement of more disk space: The more complexity and wide functionality increase the size of DBMS. Thus, it is in need of large amount of space to store and run than the traditional file system.

Additional cost of hardware: The overall cost in the installation process of database system is much more. It majorly relies on its functionality and depends on environment, size of the hardware and maintenance costs of hardware.

Cost of conversion: The overall expenditure incurred from old file-system to new database system is very high. In some scenarios, the cost of conversion is so much that the cost of DBMS and extra hardware becomes insignificant. It also includes the cost of hiring the specialized manpower and training of existing manpower to convert and run the system.

Need of additional and specialized manpower: Any organization that has the database systems, requires to hire and train its manpower on a day-to-day basis for designing and implementation of databases and to provide database administration services.

7.4. THE RELATIONAL MODEL

It is generally seen that the relational model (RM) is very simple and elegant; as already discussed, a database can be defined as collection of one or more relations, where each relation is a table with rows and columns. This tabular representation is so simple that it enables even novice users to understand the contents of a database, and it permits the use of simple, high-level languages to query the data.

Some key benefits of using the RM over the older data models are its simple data representation and the ease with which even highly complicated items can be solved.

The main construct for representing data in the RM is a relation. A relation refers to a relation instance and relation schema. The relation instance is a table, and the relation schema describes the column heads for the table.

We first explain the meaning of relation schema and then the relation instance. The schema specifies the name of relation, the name of each field (or attribute or column), and the domain of each field. A domain is referred to in a relation schema by the domain name and has a set of associated values.

7.5. FUNCTIONAL DEPENDENCY AND NORMALIZATION

Normalization is generally relied on the analysis of functional dependencies. A functional dependency is a restraint between two attributes or two sets of attributes. The key objective of the database design is to arrange the several data items into an organized structure in order to make sure that it generates set of relationships and stores the information without any repetition.

A bad database design may result into spurious and redundant data and information. Normalization refers to a technique for deciding which attributes should be grouped together in a relation. It is a tool to improve and validate a logical design, so that it satisfies various challenges that avoid redundancy of data.

In addition, Normalization refers to the process of decomposing relations with anomalies in order to produce meager, well-organized relations. Thus, it can be said that in normalization process, a relation with redundancy can be refined by replacing it or decomposing it with smaller relations that contain the identical information, but without redundancy.

In this chapter, the major area of focus is on studying the informal design guidelines for relation schemas, functional dependency as well as its types.

7.6. DE NORMALIZATION

It is an optimization technique used in the databases in which the redundant data is added to the tables. Costly joins are reduced to be used in relational databases with the help of renormalization. DE normalization is not a process of not performing normalization but it is a process performed after the normalization for database optimization.

Normalization converts the tables into more efficient ones and it decomposes one table in more tables with one form of data present in every single table. But with normalization one issue arises that the issue is that with an increased number of tables the number of joins also increases.

The issue with joins is that it has a severe impact on the performance of the database. Thus, in order to deal with this issue renormalization is performed that helps in the process of optimizing the database. It does so by adding more redundant data and also data is grouped together in a database.

When the user requires to extract some information from the database then they provide queries to the database and in turn, the database provides the users with the required results. This query-based system is an optimized process when performed in fewer tables but after normalization as the number of tables increases then queries take more time for processing as it has additional data to be processed.

DE normalization helps the relational database by reducing the inefficiencies of the database system. The query processing becomes slow in a normalized database due to the factor that various tables are created by the normalization process that stores different and related information.

The joins are used to connect the tables in a relational database, these joins make the process of a database slow. In order to deal with the issue of joins and slow processing due to normalization, the process of renormalization is considered.

Although, renormalization allows to store redundant copies of data into the tables but the DBMS system is responsible for the consistency of the data stored. Query response allows the improvement to be done in a database but here to make the data remain in a consistent form it is the job of the database designer. The consistency is reduced with the help of synchronization of redundant copies kept in the database.

As per the analysis of the renormalization process, it can be considered that the use of joins has a negative impact on the system performance of the database. Joins are used in the normalization process to make relations among different tables it is a costly process. Thus, renormalization is performed, so that performance can be enhanced.

7.6.1. Benefits of DE Normalization

DE normalization is a process of improving the database system after normalization takes place. Here the advantages of renormalization are provided:

DE normalization reduces the number of joins hence improving the database system's performance. It also reduces the number of foreign keys for tables to improve system performance. This process also helps to improve the system of the database by improving the modification time of data, by saving storage space and reducing the indexing numbers.

DE normalization also performs the function of aggregate value computation at the time of data modification and not at the selection time. The table number is reduced in renormalization that helps in performance improvement.

7.6.2. Drawbacks of DE Normalization

There are a few disadvantages of the renormalization process such as DE normalization enhances the data retrieval process but the data modification process decreases. The renormalization is an application-specific process and every time the application changes the renormalization has to be re-evaluated.

In order to optimize the database system, it increases the table size by adding more redundant data to them and in some cases, coding is simplified but in some other cases, it gets complicated.

7.7. STRUCTURED QUERY LANGUAGE (SQL)

SQL is a database operating language using which various functions of databases are performed such as database creation, any modification in the data of the database is performed. In particular, SQL is used in a relational database where the data stored are connected to each other.

SQL is used in many relational database systems such as SQL Server, Postgres, Informix, Sybase, Oracle, MS Access and MySQL. Although, there are some graphical interfaces present to work over the databases but due to their inefficiency in many cases it is very essential to have proper knowledge of SQL to be able to work in a database system.

The database management can be done efficiently with the help of SQL codes these are divided into four parts. At first, queries are performed with the help of SELECT command which is a universal command among database handlers. There is four essential working process of SELECT command such as ORDER BY, WHERE, FROM, and SELECT.

After that DML is used to perform actions such as delete data, update, and add data. DML is a subset of SELECT statement in which three major statements are used that are UPDATE, DELETE, and INSERT. There are a few control commands also used such as ROLLBACK, COMMIT, SAVEPOINT, TRANSACTION, and BEGIN.

After that DDL statements are used such as DROP, TRUNCATE, ALTER, and CREATE. These commands are helpful for indexing the structure and tables management. Then at the end data control language is used in which commands such as REVOKE and GRANT are used. These commands are useful for controlling database permission by which the database rights are managed and their grant is decided.

7.7.1. Characteristics of SQL

- **High Performance:** In a database system, there are various functions that are perfumed for the purpose of addition, deletion, and modification of data. These functions are simpler in some cases but in some other cases, they require high processing power which is provided by the SQL.

Due to the enhanced capability of performance, high processing transactions are performed with lesser efforts. There are various methods by which data can be described in an analytical form. Also, it is a structured language so it is designed for relational databases, where the number of joins is higher and thus high performance is required by the database to be provided.

- **High Availability:** There is a variety of relational databases available and all these perform with the help of SQL. The relational database works with higher efficiency when using SQL. Apart from this, there are a few other functions that the SQL performs in terms of application extension creations thus making it a powerful tool.
- **Scalability and Flexibility:** Using the SQL process of tables creation becomes very easy. Due to the availability of a lot of data, there are various tables created to store this data, but all these are not required much so it becomes essential to delete them. SQL allows these functions to be performed in a normal form and no complex procedure is required to be followed here.
- **Robust Transactional Support:** There are huge records available

in the databases and every second several transactions take place. The management of these operations is not an easy task thus, they are managed using SQL due to its efficiency to manage these operations successfully.

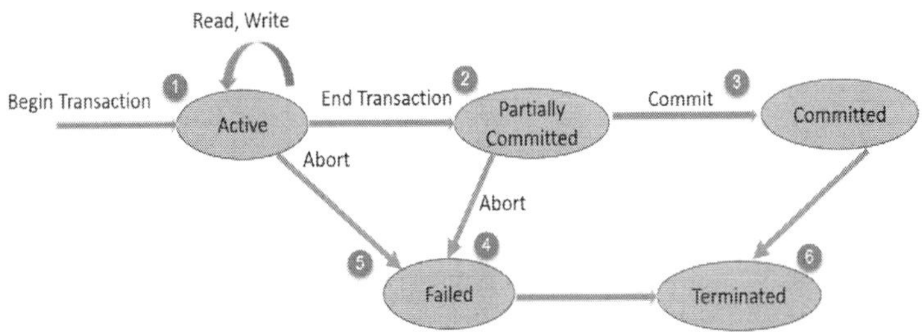

Figure 7.4:DBMS transaction management.

Source: Image by guru99.com

- **Wide Range of Application Development:** Every business of any scale requires an application and a website for their users to connect with them. The users use these platforms to perform specific functions. There are various data provided by the users every day and large data is being stored on the database of the organizations.

Now, the programmers responsible for the database creation has to use some methods to integrate the database with the website and applications. In the majority of the cases, SQL is used due to its availability on most of the database platforms and it's simple to use functional behavior.

7.7.2. Advantages of SQL

- SQL is called the high-level language due to the level of abstraction that it provides. The abstraction is an essential function to be performed as SQL allows the users to have knowledge about the data that is required from the database but not the information about the process of extracting it.
- SQL is a language that has a universal approach, for example, various functions such as data modification, delete, insert, data

access control, data query and data structures are defined using this language.

- SQL consists of portable programs and hence there moving from one database to the other is not a complex process. The porting of programs occurs very rarely only in cases such as DBMS update.

7.8. QUERY BY EXAMPLE (QBE)

In a query by example (QBE) process, the working is similar to that of a SQL but here the users are provided with a graphical interface. The database related queries can be simple and complex both, hence, QBE allows the process to be done in a graphical manner.

In major database systems QBE is allowed and it is performed in the relational database system. The graphical interface allows users to understand the process of processing how the queries are being performed.

This language allowed users to create more tables and perform more database functions. These functions have a range of operations such as creation and modification of data in a database. The only difference is the graphical interface for the insertion and deletion related database functions.

SQL is a language that has the processing power to perform complex queries, however, this processing power is also available in the QBE language but it shows the users how it's done. In the relational database, the tables are created for every type of data that is present in the database.

The joins are used to form the relationships among the tables. These joins are also used in the QBE language where the different types of data are correlated to each other. This relation allows the databases to have more efficient working.

The working of QBE is simple as the graphical interface provides tables on the screen in which users fill the criteria of selection in the tables. The simplicity of this process is visible to the user however it is not as simple as it seems. The tables present on-screen are also available in the database from where the data is retrieved.

Processing the queries manually has the issue of subjecting the database to risks. The syntax followed in QBE is of two dimensions in which the operations performed and the criteria to perform these operations are provided in tables.

Database queries in the QBE can be raised simply by typing the query in tables and the SQL commands are not required to be used. It reduces the complex procedure of SQL commands to be remembered by the user. The ending of QBE operators is represented by."" Symbol.

7.8.1. QBE Benefits

The advantages of using QBE are as follows:

QBE provides a uniform and convenient method for database control, define, update, and query. Users are not required to learn many concepts of database query and their efforts are minimized. Transactions that are covered by QBE has wide coverage but is in the simple form.

The queries are provided in the form of tables on the graphical interface. It is a non-procedural language in which no fixed process is provided to run the queries. Only the database engine before executing the syntax first checks for it.

7.9. DATABASE RECOVERY SYSTEM

There are various reasons for the failure of a computer system such as software error, power fluctuation, and disk crash, etc. Computer system failure due to any reason has a severe effect over the data stored and the information might get lost.

Thus, a database system must be able to deal with any of these situations to reduce the impact of computer failure. The properties of transactions such as durability and atomicity should be preserved. The data recovery process is performed by a recovery manager.

A database sties essentials data of the user be it an individual user or a business organization. The user is trusting the database service provider with their data. Thus, the security and protection of the data is the job of the database system.

In case of any misfortune when the data loss is inevitable, then, in that case, there are some operations being performed to ensure data safety. In order to deal with the security issues proper and efficient security protocols are implemented.

To deal with the issue of data loss, the database creates more than one copy of the data and stores it at a different location. So that in the event of computer system failure the data stored can be recovered from different locations where its copy was stored (Figure 7.5).

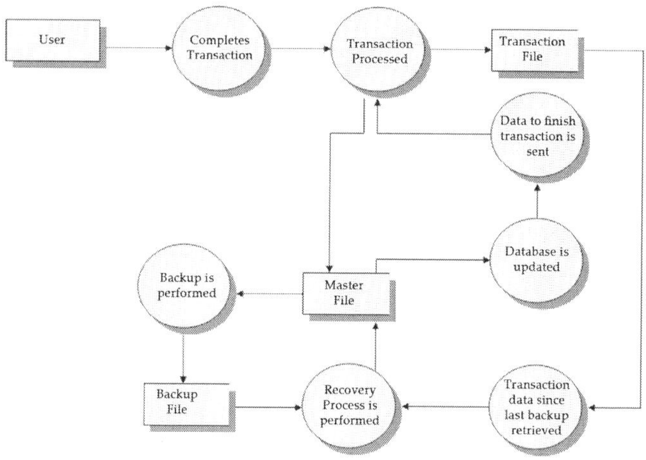

Figure 7.5: Process for database recovery.

Source: Image by Wikimedia.

7.10. QUERY PROCESSING

Query processing is the method processed in the DBMS where once the user has entered a query be it data retrieval or addition of data. Then it is processed and a strategy is developed to provide the desired results. The role of the query is only to see what data is required but it does not show how to retrieve the data.

Queries, in general, have the information related to the data retrieval so the system breaks down the query and chooses a suitable direction to follow. There are various ways to perform a query but the DBMS chooses a way that is best suited and takes less time to perform it. This is performed with the help of the query optimization process.

To execute query optimization there are two techniques available. In the first one, strategy for query execution is performed heuristic method is used to order the operations of a query. The second method of query optimization is to analyze the cost of every strategy available for the execution of the query and then chose the one with less cost.

Table 7.1: Functional Query Categories

Categorization of Functional Query			
Functional Query	**Create**	**Manage**	**Control**
	Create Statement	Insert Statement	Grant Statement
	Drop Statement	Delete Statement	Revoke Statement
	Rename Statement	Update Statement	

7.11. QUERY OPTIMIZATION

There are two factors that deal with the query performance, that are the structure of the database and query optimization strategy. The process of query optimization allows the system to work in a more efficient manner.

In query optimization, the query is converted into a format in which it can be easily accessed. For the relational queries that are of high-level DBMS evaluates the query in a systematic manner. On the basis of that analysis, certain strategies are developed for query execution and it helps in choosing the best suitable strategy for query processing.

7.11.1. Heuristic Query Optimization

It is a technique used in a DBMS where the queries are used by the users to retrieve and delete data from the database. These queries have some form of structure that is altered by the heuristic query optimization technique. To make changes to a query transformation rules are also applied so that the internal representation of the query can be changed.

Graph structure or the tree of queries are the major working factors for heuristic rules. For every query generated there is a query tree that has been created to understand the working from where the data should be retrieved. The query tree created at the initial phase is converted to an efficient tree with the help of transformation rules.

7.11.2. Cost-Based Query Optimization

The cost-based query optimization technique is an effective technique to deal with the issue of processing time in the database management system. A DBMS applies the query optimization technique to make the queries process in lesser time and with lesser complexity. Here the cost-based query optimization is described.

Cost-based query optimization is a technique in which the optimizer evaluates the cost of every strategy by which a query can provide results. Out of which the most suitable strategy is selected. The strategy is selected based on various factors such as lower complexity in processing the query request, time taken by the query to be processed and the resources required to deal with the query.

The major factor on which the query cost focus is the selectivity that means input relation quantity forming output. The main factors responsible for cost query determination are secondary storage access cost, storage cost, cost of computation, cost of memory usage and cost of communication.

The secondary storage access cost includes the cost of operation of database manipulation. In the database manipulation process, different factors are incorporated such as actions performed on a data block present on secondary memory, these actions are reading writing and searching.

Searching of data blocks cost is dependent on the index type, for example, the index could be hashed index, secondary index or primary index. There are other factors also present that impact the data block searching cost such as the required data block could be present in a single block or it is scattered at different locations of a disk.

The cost of storage is the cost related to using storage to store the results generated in response to the queries. The cost of computation mainly deals with the aspects of computation performed while responding to a query. There are some functions performed at the time of query processing such as records searching, filed value computation, records merging, records sorting ion a file. Data buffers are used to perform these functions.

The cost of memory usage is very simple it only includes the cost of the number of memory buffers used for the execution of a query. The cost of communication includes the cost of the different processes such as query transfer and the end place where the query result is provided.

That means, in communication, the query is generated by the user which is provided to the database and the DBMS processes the query and provides the result of the query to the user. Communication also deals with processing the queries and showing results to the user.

On comparison of all the costs, the most important is the secondary storage access cost as the processing of secondary storage is slower. In small databases the data files are available in the memory, thus, the computation cost is minimized by the optimizer.

In the case of large databases, the computation cost is not minimized rather secondary storage access cost is minimized by the optimizer and in case of distributed database again communication cost is reduced as the data transfer is done with the help of different sites.

Execution strategies cost is estimated with the help of optimizer. DBMS catalog stores the statistical data which is accessed by the optimizer for cost estimation of executing processes. The information that is being stored in a database management system is provided as:

Number of records in relation X: – R

Number of blocks required to store relation X: – B

Blocking factor of relation X: – BFR

Number of levels for each multi-level index for an attribute A: – IA

Number of first-level index blocks for an attribute A: – BAI1

Selection cardinality of attribute A in relation R: – SA

The selectivity of the attributes: – SLA

$SA = R \times SLA$

7.12. DATABASE TUNING

Database tuning (DT) is a process in which various activities are performed to optimize the database and the standardized database performance. DoS allows the database to perform in a manner that increases the use of available resources to a maximized level.

Every database system is created in such a manner that it can work efficiently but still with the help of various processes the database can be tuned top perform more efficiently. This tuning can be done by7 customizing different settings of a database.

7.13. DATA MIGRATION

The process of data migration includes the transfer of data from one space to the other such as data transfer among computers, formats, and storage types. The process of data migration is very essential for a DBMS in order to transfer the data from one space to the other in a computer system.

Different repositories have data stored in them and it becomes an essential process to transfer data from one repository to the other, this job is done with the help of data migration techniques. There are a few things that should be considered for efficient data migration.

These aspects are that different applications have different types of data stored in them. Thus, if a data is migrated from one application to the other then it is essential to consider it to first transform the data in accordance with the application on which it is getting migrated.

Data migration is considered to be the time taking process but it compensates it by providing various benefits. For data migration, it is not required to maintain older applications.

7.14. CONCLUSION

The database management is an essential program created to manage database operations. There are a lot of operations performed on a database and in order for them to work efficiency a management system is developed known as DBMS.

There are different forms of databases available but the most used database is the relational database in which the data is stored in a structured manner. The operations such as data retrieval, data insertion, and data modification are performed over a database. For this, the query is used by the users to retrieve data from the databases.

There is a SQL created to deal with the queries in the DBMS system. The SQL queries are used for data retrieval in an efficient manner and the SQL allows the data processing to be done with enhanced efficiency.

REFERENCES

1. Bhardwaj, A., & Sharma, K., (2015). *Types of Queries in Database System.* [online] Researchgate.net. Available at: https://www.researchgate.net/publication/303313899_Types_of_Queries_in_Database_System (accessed on 1 June 2020).
2. Gupta, S., & Mittal, A., (2017). *Introduction to Database Management System* (2nd edn.). London: University Science Press.
3. Guru99.com. (n.d.). *What is DBMS? Application, Types, Example, Advantages, Disadvantages.* [online] Available at: https://www.guru99.com/what-is-dbms.html (accessed on 1 June 2020).
4. Intellipaat Blog, (2019). *Features of SQL-SQL Tutorial -Intellipaat.* [online] Available at: https://intellipaat.com/blog/tutorial/sql-tutorial/sql-features/ (accessed on 1 June 2020).
5. Kahate, A., (2004).*Introduction to Database Management Systems.* Pearson Education India.
6. MariaDB Knowledge Base, (n.d.). *Understanding DE Normalization.* [online] Available at: https://mariadb.com/kb/en/understanding-denormalization/ (accessed on 1 June 2020).
7. Martin, R., (n.d.). *Database Quotes (10 quotes).* [online] Goodreads.com. Available at: https://www.goodreads.com/quotes/tag/database (accessed on 1 June 2020).
8. Ramarkrishnan, R., & Gehrke, J., (2004). *Database Management System.* (2nd edn.) London: McGraw-Hill Pub. Co. (ISE Editions).
9. Techopedia.com. (2011). *What is Data Definition Language (DDL)?-Definition from Techopedia.* [online] Available at: https://www.techopedia.com/definition/1175/data-definition-language-ddl (accessed on 1 June 2020).
10. Techopedia.com. (2016). *What is Structured Query Language (SQL)?-Definition from Techopedia.* [online] Available at: https://www.techopedia.com/definition/1245/structured-query-language-sql (accessed on 1 June 2020).
11. Thakur, S., (2018). *Explain Data Manipulation Language (DML) with Examples in DBMS.* [online] Whatisdbms.com. Available at: https://whatisdbms.com/explain-data-manipulation-language-with-examples-in-dbms/ (accessed on 1 June 2020).

CHAPTER 8

Data Warehousing and Data Mining

CONTENTS

8.1. Introduction 204
8.2. Characteristics of Data Warehouse And Data Mining 206
8.3. Working Process of Data Warehouse 207
8.4. Working Process of Data Mining 208
8.5. Advantages of Data Warehouse And Data Mining 213
8.6. Limitations of Data Warehouse And Data Mining 216
8.7. Olap Vs Oltp 218
8.8. Automatic Clustering Detection 221
8.9. Data Mining With Neural Networks 223
8.10. Conclusion 228
References 229

Data warehousing and data mining are essential concepts of the distributed database system. A data warehouse collects and stores the data of the business organization from all of its functionalities such as sales, marketing, finance, production, and human resource. The data mining is the process of analyzing the data collected and provide relevant information from the huge chunk of data. This chapter initially provides information regarding the characteristics, working, and different aspects of data warehouse and data mining. The data processing is done with the help of OLTP and OLAP processes in data warehouse and data mining, these concepts have been described in the chapter. In the end, neural networks have been described in relation to the data mining process.

8.1. INTRODUCTION

Data warehousing is a technique used by a business organization to analyze the data collected from various sources. There are various sources from where the data related to business functionalities are generated and the analysis of this data helps an organization to develop future business strategies.

A data warehouse (DW) is not a database rather it is the collection of various databases so that data analysis can be performed for a business organization. The DW is a type of analytical database which is accounted for the analysis process. The data stored in a DW is present in a structured manner so that analysis can be done in an efficient manner.

Meaningful business insights can be generated with the help of the data warehousing process. Various heterogeneous sources are clubbed together in a DW and store data in a systematic manner. For a business organization, a DW is an essential tool of business insights system that provides reporting and analysis of data.

The data stored in a DW is collected from various functions of a business such a sale, marketing, human resource, resource management, production, distribution, and research and development. In simple terms, the DW collects data from various sources and transforms it into a systematic manner so that it can be used for the analysis of data.

The major difference between a DW and database is the processing technique in both. In the DW, the OLAP technique is used for processing which is online analytical processing (OLAP), while in a database the OLTP is used which online transaction is processing.

The data mining (DM) process as the name suggests is a process by which collected data in the warehouse is analyzed to form some important results. Future behavior analysis is performed with the help of the DM process. The hidden patterns are observed with the help of DM and it mines the data from valuable sources.

In the case of an e-commerce business, there is a bunch of data that is collected and stored in a DW. In most cases it stores data related to consumer behavior such as the time spent by the customer over the website, buying patterns over the customer, product searches, etc.

On the basis of this data a person, specific service is provided to every customer in which they are provided with related search results, discounted products and products as per individual's buying capacity. The DM practice is utilized to draw data patterns; however, the sole purpose of a DW is to provide analysis for the business.

In distributed database architecture the OLTP, i.e., online transaction processing is used in which the transactions in terms of information exchange are processed. The OLTP approach is used in order to manage the transactions that are done to and from the database. On the other hand, OLAP, i.e., OLAP is an approach used in the data warehousing so that proper data analysis can be done in a structured format.

These processes of DW and DM are getting their foothold in the information system as it helps the organization in business development and strategic decision making. OLAP technique is mainly used for analysis and not processing.

The major advantage of the DW is that it helps business organizations to store and analyze a large amount of data related to their business in a structured form. The DW is an integrated system within an organization so that whenever the requirement arises for the data analysis it can be accessed easily with insightful results.

The DM process gathers data from the DW and analyzes it for insightful information gathering in terms of business strategy development. There are different architectures of DW present such as star, snowflake, and constellation schema. One of the major aspects of a warehouse architecture is the granularity that determines the data detailing in data. The volume of data stored is directly affected by granularity.

8.2. CHARACTERISTICS OF DATA WAREHOUSE AND DATA MINING

8.2.1. Data Warehouse Characteristics

The characteristics of a DW are that a DW is subject-oriented, integrated, time-variant, and non-volatile. The characteristics can be described as:

- **Subject Oriented:** The DW is known to provide information related to a specific subject such as sales, marketing, distributions, etc. and are not affected by the ongoing process of a company.
- **Integrated:** The integration refers to a system in which the data is stored in a way that is easily acceptable. The data is collected from a variety of heterogeneous sources such as level documents, databases, etc. Integration in terms of DW is that it collects data from different sources and presents in a similar manner and format so that at the time of analysis required data can be easily acquired.

The integration process can be understood from an example in which a similar type of data is stored at three different databases. The data that is stored in these are gender, date, and balance which are stored in different formats in all three databases. However, when the data is required from the DW it is transformed and cleaned and the format of data from all different sources is provided in a single format.

- **Time-Variant:** This characteristic of the DW shows that data is present in the DW with a timestamp in terms of month or year attached. This allows the warehouse to provide information related to collected data in a historical manner. There is an issue with the DW is that once data is stored in it, no change or alteration can be performed on it.
- **Non-Volatile:** When new data is allowed to store in a warehouse than it does not delete the previous data. This aspect is beneficial for the organization as it helps them understand the change in customer's approach towards their business.

The DW does not allow the update, delete, and insert feature in it. There are only two operations can be performed namely, data loading and data access. These operations allow the DW to perform only the data storage and no altercation can be performed which allows the analysis process to be done in an efficient manner.

8.2.2. Data Mining Characteristics

The approach used in the process of DM is the information gathering in which the relevant information is analyzed with the help of collected data. The DM characteristics are:

- Increased data quantity

In the previous approach of DM data limited to the industry was collected but in the current scenario, there are various technologies available that have enhanced this process to a much greater extent. Nowadays, techniques such as machine learning and big data have been integrated that is useful for the collection for a huge amount of data irrespective of the industry of working.

This process is useful for the business organization due to an increase in the data collected from various sources that are being collected from sources such as sales, marketing, development, and production functions within a business. All this data is analyzed to acquire useful information for the business strategy development process.

- Noisy Data Collection

There is a huge cluster of incomplete data which is provided to the DM. There are a large variety of techniques used in DM process that analyses this data and provide relevant information by predicting from given information.

- Complexity in Data Structure

The data is provided in all forms and types either structured or unstructured and thus it the data structure is a bit complicated for the system. The process of conventional statistical analysis cannot be used here due to the complexity of the data structure.

8.3. WORKING PROCESS OF DATA WAREHOUSE

The system of the DW is useful for the storage of data as well as reporting on them. At first, there are multiple systems of data storage are used which after going through the process of extraction, transformation, and loading go to the DW where it gets stored for the long term and from time to time it gets analyzed as well.

After the analysis of the stored data, it is presented to the different departments of business as per their requirements. This data is presented in forms such as reporting, visualization, and business insights. The working of a DW is very simple it is just a storage space of a huge chunk of data collected from various sources for the purpose of analysis.

The working if the DW is dependent on the type of organization of working, it is also dependent on the complexity of the organization in which it is being implemented. But mostly the processes that are being followed are similar like at first the collected data go through the cleansing process.

This process of data cleansing is not considered the part of the DW as it is just the process of arranging collected data in a structured format. This is, thus, known as the integration layer. After this process, the collected data is saved in the DW.

After that, with the help of an access layer, the data stored in a structured form is provided to the applications that needed that data. The structure of data collected in the DW is governed by an additional layer in a DW which is called the metadata. This metadata has information related to the data collected in the DW (Figure 8.1).

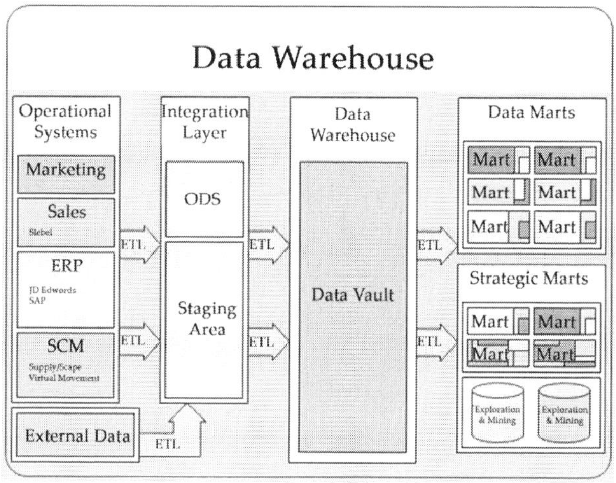

Figure 8.1: Data warehouse.

Source: Image by Wikipedia.

8.4. WORKING PROCESS OF DATA MINING

There is a huge amount of data present for a business organization that is collected from different functionalities of the business. This data is useful when proper information can be gathered from it. This is where the DM process is useful as it extracts insightful information for the businesses.

There is a wide range of applications that uses the DM approach in the industry.

The application area of DM is scattered to risk management, corporate analysis, fraud inspection, business management, and market analysis. Here the steps in the DM process are provided that are data cleaning, data integration, data transformation, data discretion, data presentation, and pattern evaluation. Figure 8.2 shows the process involved in a DM process.

Figure 8.2: Aspects of data mining.

8.4.1. Data Cleaning

Data cleaning as the name suggests is a procedure to remove inaccurate data that is present in the storage system. This process is of utmost importance because if the data present in the database and record set is incomplete then the final analysis will get affected and the results will be less useful.

There are some processes that are being applied for the data cleaning such as ignoring the tuple in which the missing record is left or not considered. This method is, however, is limited to the tuples with less amount of missing values as if there is a tuple with a huge amount of missing data then it will cause issues in the result.

Apart from that missing values can be filled manually but it is applicable for a data set that is limited. Another approach is to fill the missing values with the global values that serve the same purpose as the missing value. One last resort is to fill the missing values with the predicted value that is the attributed mean value.

8.4.2. Data Integration

Data integration is a technique of merging data collected from various sources into the one DW in which previous information is merged together with the newly collected information. As a DW does not altercate the previous data so it becomes an easy process to integrate previous and new data.

In the process of data integration, two major processes involved are tight and lose coupling. Both of these will be discussed in this section:

- **Tight Coupling**: In this approach data from various sources is collected and after going through the ETL process it is stored at a single physical location.
- **Loose Coupling**: It has a different approach from tight coupling, here data is kept at the original database source. A combination is used in which the user-generated queries are taken and are converted to a format that is readily understood by the source database and using that the server database obtains the result and sends it back to the user.

8.4.3. Data Transformation

In this process, the data is collected in one format and is converted to a different format which is majorly done so that data can be understood by all the processes involved. Mostly the data conversion is considered in this process but in some cases, one computer program is converted from one language to the other so that different programs can authorize it and the program can run on different platforms.

Data transformation can be achieved by different strategies like smoothing, attribute construction, normalization, generalization, and aggregation. Smoothing allows to remove noise from data, in aggregation aggregate values are given to the data, in the generalization process hierarchy climbing is considered where the high level and low-level data are replaced with each other and in the normalization as the name suggests attributes are normalized to a scalable range.

8.4.4. Data Discretization

The continuous attribute domain is divided into intervals with the help of a technique called data discretization. Small labels of the interval are used to restore values of study attributes. This process is helpful for the purpose of knowledge level representation of the data collected from the DM process, it shows the data in a compact and easy manner. There are two essential processes followed in data discretization namely, top-down, and bottom-up discretization.

- **Top-Down Discretization**: In this process, points that are found first are used so that the entire attribute range can be divided, after that for resulting intervals the loops of divided data are used.
- **Bottom-Up Discretization**: In this process, continuous values are considered as split points, some of them are removed by integrating values of the neighborhood intervals.

8.4.5. Concept Hierarchy

Concept hierarchy is used for data reduction, in which data is first collected and then the low-level concept and high-level concepts are replaced with each other. Concept hierarchies define multiple abstraction levels of a multi-dimensional model in which the data is stored in multiple dimensions. This abstraction allows users with a different perspective with the flexibility to view the data.

The DM process performed for a data set that is reduced has fewer operations of input and output and has enhanced mining as compared to the mining of large data set. Thus, due to the benefits associated with these processes the concept hierarchy and discretization are not used during mining instead they are used before the DM process.

In concept hierarchy mapping sequences are defined from low level to high-level concepts. In order to understand concept hierarchy, take an example of applying concept hierarchy for dimension location. For this take city values as Chicago, New York, Vancouver, and Toronto.

Here, the cities can be mapped to the state to which they belong like Chicago can be mapped to Illinois and Vancouver to British Columbia. Further, these states can be mapped to the countries they belong to. Here, concept hierarchy is formed with the help of mapping, this process mapped the low-level concepts of cities to the high-level concept of countries.

So, this data reduction allowed the DM process to perfume lesser action as the cities are already mapped to the countries. Thus, the analysis can be performed much easier and the system will only have to look for the country and not every province and state to which the city belongs.

The database schema already has various concept hierarchy. The set grouping hierarchy is created in which the attributes of a given dimension are grouped together forming a group of similar values, this is also a part of concept hierarchy.

The process of concept hierarchy formation done manually will be a time-consuming task. This issue is resolved database schema already has some hierarchies. Concept hierarchy allows the data to be more in detail and the data is transformed into multiple granular levels.

8.4.6. Pattern Evaluation and Data Presentation

After collecting and analyzing the data, the major and most essential process is to represent the data. If the data that is represented in a manner that the customers and users can understand then only, they are able to use the data as per their requirement.

The data representation is not of a much issue for the experienced users but if the users and clients are not experienced in the statistical field then it becomes very crucial to present the data in simpler forms such as graphs and diagrams. The methods used to represent the economic data are provided below:

- Cartography;
- Frequency distribution graphs;
- One dimensional;
- Pictographs;
- Plain graphs;
- Three-dimensional diagrams;
- Time-series graphs; and
- Two dimensional.

8.5. ADVANTAGES OF DATA WAREHOUSE AND DATA MINING

8.5.1. Data Warehouse Advantages

There is a common goal to every organization which they all share that is better decision making for their business. There are various ways in which the DW can benefit the organization after it is being integrated into the business intelligence framework. The advantages of the DW are:

- **Enhanced Business Intelligence**: The information can be accessed from various sources that allow the decision-makers to have plenty of data available regarding making business decisions. To a business process, a DW can be applied in an effortless manner to every business functionality such as financial management, inventory, risk, sales, and market segmentation.
- **Time-Saving**: In a DW the information is collected and saved from various sources that help in integrating and merging all types of data. Critical data is provided to all the users that help them in the decision-making process which is done in an informed way. Also, the executives are not dependent on the IT support as they can query data easily and thus this process helps in saving time and money for the organization.
- **Data Quality and Consistency Enhancement**: Multiple sources of data are used to convert it into a format that is consistent. As the data is in a standard form available across the organization so every department produces consistent results. Thus, solid decision making is performed due to the availability of accurate data.
- **High Return on Investment is Generated**: The organizations that have implemented the DW into their business functions have higher cost-saving and revenue generation as compared to the organization that does not use the DW.
- **Competitive Advantage**: This is the major factor that all the business organizations require so that their business remains above then their rivals in the industry. A complete view of the organization's current standing is provided by the DW. It allows the companies to analyze the areas of risk and opportunity for their business and thus they can start working in the weaker

This process allows organizations to increase their revenue by increasing sales. This is done with the help of target market accumulation. Allows the customer to have more options of product to choose from, thus, helping the organization to generate more revenues.

- **Future Trend Prediction:** DM techniques use current and historical data to analyze and extract information. This helps the organization to have a better idea of the changes that the business went through and thus helps in the prediction of future business trends.

This is done with the help of analyzing customer data and it also analyses the behavioral changes that the customers have over time in terms of demanding the services and goods. This data analysis helps the companies to predict the services that customers require now and may want in the future.

8.6. LIMITATIONS OF DATA WAREHOUSE AND DATA MINING

8.6.1. Data Warehouse Limitations

DW works as a data analysis tool that accumulates data from various functionalities of a business, being a relational database, it stores the collected data at one data store. The updating process of data in the DW is not as real-time transactional data storing rather it is an end of the day batch job. One of the major advantages of a DW is to provide timelier and better data to mangers so that using this data hey can make efficient strategic decisions. Although there are various advantages associated with the DW but at the same time, it has some drawbacks also which have been described in this section.

- **Extra Reporting Work:** There is an issue of extra working for different departments of a business which varies with the size of the organization. Every data type that is required in a DW is required to be provided by the IT department of every business division.

Sometimes this process is very simple in which only data is to be copied from the existing databases. But at other times it becomes very hectic and time-consuming because the data is required to be gathered from customers that are not present already in the database but it is required for efficient analysis.

- **Cost/Benefit Analysis:** Cost/Benefit analysis is one of the major disadvantages of the DW. Being an IT project there is a huge requirement of man hours and money for the development of a tool which is in many cases does not get properly used so that its implementation cost can be justified.

Apart from that, the warehouse is required to be maintained and updated with the growth of the business so that all the business-related data can be stored. It, however, provides relevant data for strategic business development which is beneficial for the organization but in many cases, the cost of maintaining such a DW is not justified by the amount of profit it generates.

- **Data Ownership Concerns:** A DW in many cases is a type of cloud service that too implemented as software as a service. Thus, the data stored over this platform has some security concern that it is dependent on the loyalty and trust factor for the cloud service provider.

Even in case, the data is stored in a local environment still it has the issue of data access. If the employees with access to the data stored in the ware house may leak the data. Thus, it is extremely important that the data analysis performed by the employees of the organization should be the most trusted once.

It is important because there is a user's personal data is also stored over the DW. In case this data leaks than the customer's trust over the business reduced and the organization loses its value among the customers.

- **Data Flexibility:** The data sets present in a DW are static and thus it does not have the required ability to find a specific solution. The data is stored over the DW and it remains there for a good amount of time thus, historic data is stored in the DW.

This is the reason why when data filtering is approached it is days or weeks old. In addition to that, the query speed and processing speed are hard to tune due to the ad hoc queries that it goes through. All these issues reduce data flexibility over the DW.

8.6.2. Data Mining Limitations

The tools for DM are very powerful and it is not very easy for an inexperienced person to handle. The data preparation is required to be done by a skilled person with experience in this field. The data preparation and output analysis are also done by an experienced person.

Different patterns are extracted by the DM techniques and the relationship among them is identified by the professional executive. This data is to be presented in a format that could be easily understood by the users. Thus, to perform all these functions a skilled worker is required.

- **Privacy Issues:** Privacy issues are inevitable in the DM technique. This technique is implemented in the business organization to extract data from all the functionality of the business that are sales, marketing, production, and human resource.

In this process, the collected data also involves personal data of the user which is required to be maintained by the business organization. There are various factors using which the DM techniques work, it may sometime violate user privacy. Thus, user safety and security are at risk in this process.

- **Security Issues:** One of the major issues with all the data-oriented technology is user security. There are various organizations that have the user's personal data such as payroll, birthday, and social security number, etc. All these user related data are very confidential and is required to be securely stored by the organization.

There were various cases in which the organization's data was breached and hackers were able to attack over the data storage to gain access to the user's data. Various big enterprises have been subjected to this attack time and again which has caused them huge money and trust value in the market.

- **Misuse of Information:** The DM system has very little measures for data security. Thus, the issue of information misuse increases and the hackers can use this information to harm the user. Thus, it is extremely important that the security measured should be updated for DM techniques so that the instances of data theft can be reduced.

8.7. OLAP VS OLTP

8.7.1. Online Transaction Processing System

In OLTP processing, the alterations in the database are done in real time. Processes such as update, insertion, and deletion are recorded as they happen and this is the major focus of the system of OLTP. Queries in the OLTP system are shorter and simpler in processing and takes less processing time on top of that the space required is also less.

The database is frequently updated in the OLTP system. There are high chances of transactions being rejected in the middle of the processing that may have an adverse impact on data integrity. Thus, it is very essential to maintain data integrity in the OLTP system.

The tables in the OLTP database are in the 3 normal form (3NF) form such that they are in normalized form. In order to understand an OLTP system is the automated teller machine (ATM) that performs shorter transactions and the modification is done in the account status. It is the data source for an OLAP system (Figure 8.3)

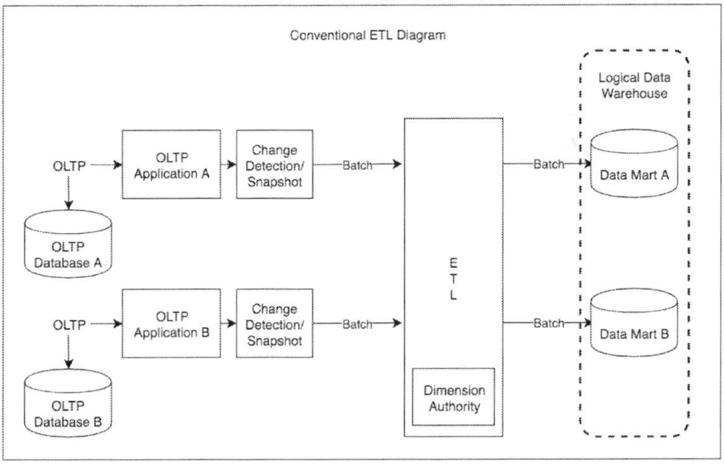

Figure 8.3: The online transaction processing system.

Source: Image by Wikipedia.

8.7.2. Online Analytical Processing System

In the OLAP database, historical data is stored which is provided by the OLTP system. The users of the OLAP system are allowed to view the multi-dimensional data summarized in different summaries. OLAP also allows the users to extract data using a huge database and then they can perform analysis over it for the purpose of decision making.

OLAP allows its users to have multidimensional data extraction by executing complex queries. As OLTP has the issue of transactions declining in the middle, the data integrity remains intact as the OLAP system is used by the user for data retrieval from a huge database for analysis purposes. It is a simple process; the user only has to input the query one more time and the data will be extracted.

There are longer transactions that are to be performed in the OLAP system and hence time and space requirement is comparatively high. The frequency of transactions in an OLAP system is lesser than an OLTP system. Apart from these OLAP databases do not have tables in the normalized form in the database like the OLTP database. Examples of an OLAP system are to view sales reports, marketing management, budgeting, and financial report (Figure 8.4).

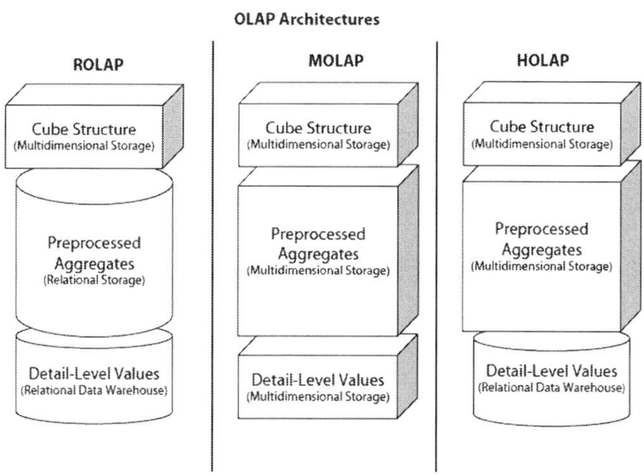

Figure 8.4: Online analytical processing system.

Source: Image by Wikimedia.

8.7.3. Major Differences in OLAP and OLTP Systems

Both these systems have their own advantages and disadvantages and they have their own working which is some cases dependent on each other. There are some differences also present in both of them, the major difference in these two have been described here:

- Due to higher transactional frequency in OLTPs in the event of failed transactions in the middle of processing than it harms the data integrity. However, in the case of OLAP, the frequency of transactions is lesser and thus data integrity does not get affected due to failed transactions.

- The frequency of transactions in an OLTP is high but in an OLAP it is less.
- Major operations performed by an OLTP is an insertion, updating, and deletion. However, OLAP's major attributes are to acquire data in the multidimensional form for the purpose of analysis.
- A major point of difference between the two is that OLTP is a system of online transactions such as ATM and OLAP is a system of data extraction and analysis such as financial reporting and sales reports.
- OLAP takes more time for processing than an OLTP system.
- OLTP database stores data in a normalized form that is in third normalized form while tables are not stored in a normalized format in an OLAP database.
- Queries of an OLAP have high complexity as compared to an OLTP system.
- The data which is in the form of online transaction is the data source for an OLTP system, however, databases of OLTP are data source of the OLAP system.
- The size of transactions in an OLTP is short whereas in OLAP it is long.

8.8. AUTOMATIC CLUSTERING DETECTION

8.8.1. Searching for Clusters

In the DM process training sets that are pre-classified are used and a model is developed for them that helps in predicting the classification of the new record. However, in the clustering process, pre-classified data sets are not available and the dependent and independent variables are not provided separately.

Rather, in the clustering process record groups are searched that contains similar information such as users with similar requirements and the products with similar functionalities are grouped together. Automatic cluster detection is not performed alone as it is not an end process.

Once the clusters are identified than with the help of other methods it is detected that what these clusters represent. This technique shows results that are useful in terms of identifying the data sets with a similar working process.

One example of cluster detection can be seen from the astrologers' research of stellar evolution in which stars were focused as major objects of data. The stars were grouped together based on their luminosity and temperatures. The research showed that the stars were grouped in different clusters depending on the stellar life cycle phases.

8.8.2. Strengths of Automatic Cluster Detection

The major aspects of strength for automatic cluster detection are that it provides unsupervised knowledge discovery, it provides optimal results for textual, numeric, and categorical data, it is easy to apply and also it is unsupervised.

This type of cluster detection is undirected, which means it has not a requirement for application and thus it can be applied without having prior knowledge of internal database structure. It has the ability to identify hidden structure which is useful for performance improvement of directed techniques.

The automatic cluster detection can be applied to a diverse range of data types. Any type of data can be subjected to automatic cluster detection with the help of different distance measures. It is very useful in terms of financial data clustering.

In most of the techniques for cluster detection, it is not required to massage input data for every single instance rather very few massaging is required. Also, particular fields are not required to be identified as inputs and outputs.

8.8.3. Weaknesses of Automatic Cluster Detection

There is some weakness associated with automatic cluster detection such as difficulty in identifying right distance weights and measures, it is sensitive to initial parameters and the interpretation of resulting clusters is also complex.

For automatic cluster detection, it becomes very hard to allocate distance metrics as the variables that are present in the cluster can be present in a mixture. The distance Metrix allocation is the most important process to be followed as it is the similarity measure that determines the cluster formation and the data in the cluster are stored on the basis of this Metrix.

For disparate types of variables, appropriate weighting schemes are difficult to determine. It also has the issues relate to the initial parameters that have been determined initially. In case if the initial parameters do not satisfy the natural data structure than the technique will not be able to provide efficient results.

Although the automatic cluster detection discovers data in an unsupervised form which is considered to be a strength for the technique. However, the issue with this is that the user will not be able to know what to look for, thus there are high chances of missing important values. Thus, the identified clusters will not have practical value.

8.9. DATA MINING WITH NEURAL NETWORKS

In decision support systems and DM approaches artificial neural networks are beneficial. There is a wide range of implementation of neural networks for various industries. These applications include medical condition diagnosis, financial series identification, valuable customer cluster identification, fraudulent credit card transaction identification, recognition of numbers written on checks and prediction of engine failure rates.

According to Alex Berson, "we can define information as that which resolves uncertainty. We can further say that the decision-making is the progressive resolution of uncertainty, and is a key to a purposeful behavior."

People generalize the data based on their experience of doing it, however, in the case of computers they are bound to follow explicit instructions again and again. A neural network is helpful in this context as they fill this gap with the help of modeling. The efficiency of the neural network enhances when they are used in a well-defined domain.

The neural network has the ability to generalize and learn from available data and when subjected to the well-defined domain they act as humans learn from experience. Due to this ability, neural networks are very useful for DM processes. It reduces the time consumption for data generalization.

Table 8.1: Functions and Models of Neural Network

Model	Training-Paradigm	Topology	Primary-Functions
Kohonen feature map	Unsupervised	Feed-forward	Clustering
Temporal difference learning	Reinforcement	Feed-forward	Time-series
Probabilistic neural networks	Supervised	Feed-forward	Classification
Recurrent back propagation	Supervised	Limited	Modeling, time-series
Back propagation	Supervised	Feed-forward	Classification, modeling, time-series
Adaptive resonance theory	Unsupervised	Recurrent	Clustering
Learning vector quantization	Supervised	Feed-forward	Classification
Radial basis function networks	Supervised	Feed-forward	Classification, modeling, time-series
ARTMAP	Supervised	Recurrent	Classification

Source: Table from Data Warehousing OLAP and Data Mining by Nagabhushana.

8.9.1. Neural Networks for Data Mining

The input provided to a neural processing element is given by connected elements of processing. Weighted connection works as a pass filter that either intensifies a signal or reduces it. For the element of neural processing total input is given by summing up the total input signal that the element receives.

The output signal ranges between 0 and 1 which the result of a mathematical function via which the total input signal passes. The output is not digital but analog in nature. When the weight of connection and input signal matches the output is near to 1. But if there is no resemblance in the input signal and connection weights the output is considered to be 0.

Intermediate values are used to represent the varying similarity degrees. The neural processing can be forced to make a decision in the binary format but more information can be retained using analog signals within 0.0 to 1.0 range. The output provided in this range provides more information for the succeeding layer of neural processing. So, it is evident that neural networks working is similar to that of analog computers.

8.9.2. Neural Network Topologies

The neural network's processing capabilities are profoundly impacted by interconnections and the neural processing unit's arrangement. The network topology in neural networks is the connection of neurons which is an essential factor for network functioning and learning.

There are some hidden processing units that collect input units from other layers of processing units. The output of previous processing units provides inputs to the succeeding layer that works in parallel to each other.

The final result provided by the computation of the neural network is converted to a processing unit set and is called to be output units. The data flow among the hidden, input, and output units of processing are defined with the help of three main connection topologies. These major connection topologies are feed forward, fully, and limited recurrent network.

8.9.3. Feed-Forward Networks

Feed forward neural networks are also known as deep feed forward networks. The major working of the fed forward neural network is function approximation. The special cases of feed forward neural networks are convolutional and recurrent neural networks.

In these networks, the result that the system is required to achieve is pre-determined, the major job if these networks are to define what the system should do and the system learns this by running a similar program time and again.

In a feed forward network, all the information is fed to the neural network. This type of neural network has unidirectional working and the result is dependent on the set of input provided initially. In the neural network, data is entered through input units. Input values are the unit activation values that are assigned to the output values.

Connection weights are the major identifiers for the output values and that are magnified in case connection weight are more than 1.0 and positive. The output values are diminished when the connection weights are between 0.0 and 1.0. In case of negative connection weights magnification or diminishing of the signal is performed in the opposite direction.

There is an aggregation of the threshold value and a combination of all units of input, and that value is provided by the processing units. In the multi-layer network, every layer gets input from the previous layer, why are the outputs of the previous. This output is a value provided by some activation function through which the total input signal is passed.

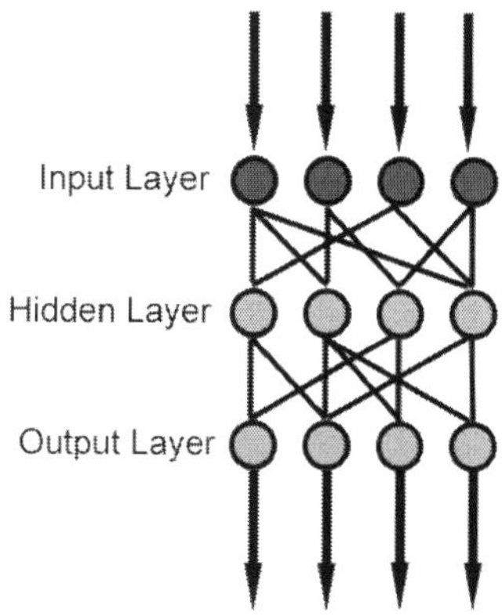

Figure 8.5: Feed forward neural network.

Source: Image by Wikipedia.

The logistic function is considered to be the most complicated activation function to be used in the neural network. The logistic activation function alters the input value provided to a range of 0 to 1 as the output value. The threshold weight that is provided here is of utmost importance as on the basis of that the curve is shifted either right or left.

On the basis of the threshold weight's sign, the activation function has the ability to change the output value higher or lower. The data flow in a neural network is not as simple as flowing from input to the output layer as there are some hidden layers present, there can be a number of hidden layers present.

In most cases of the neural networks, the units of every layer are connected to each other, this can visualize as the nervous system of humans where neurons are connected to each other and data flows among them in case of decision making.

This is not a case of a feed forward network; the connection weights can be lesser if the construction of connection and weights are done based on a pre-determined rule. In the case of a neural network, some techniques are present that help in reducing the unnecessary weights even after training of the neural network.

If the connection weights are lesser than the data processing will be faster which will make the working of the network even faster. The generalization of hidden inputs is also done in an enhanced manner. Feed forward is not any activation function rather it is the connection topology definition.

8.9.4. Limited Recurrent Networks

The recurrent neural networks are the ones in which the input of the next layer is provided by the output of the previous layer. In recurrent networks, the information is already provided to the network where the input sequence is important. Here, records of prior inputs are stored in the neural network and these are factored for producing solutions.

In simple, language the neural network collects and stores all the data from every layer so that learning from this data the network can provide an efficient solution to a given problem. The benefit of a recurrent network is that past inputs are also provided and they are mixed with current inputs so that hidden information can be generated. This intermixing is done with the help of feedback connections.

Thus, the neural network contains previous inputs in a memory with the help of activations. There are two main architectures present for recurrent networks that are limited. Elman (1990), suggested context units that are feedback received from hidden units which are provided to the additional input set.

Jordan (1986) previously suggested using the feedback provided by output units to the context units. However, the recurrence of this type can be considered to be a negotiation among the complexity of the fully recurrent neural network and simplicity of a neural network that is fed forward due to the factor that it allows back propagation training algorithm.

8.9.5. Fully Recurrent Networks

The fully recurrent network was developed in the 1980s and has the ability to learn sequences that are temporal. This learning is either online or in batch mode. There are two layers present in fully recurrent networks that are output and input layer.

Adjustable weights are applied for the connection of input layer units and output layer units. Every unit is provided with an activation function that is time varying and real valued in nature. Fully recurrent networks learn by mapping the input sequences to the output sequences.

8.10. CONCLUSION

A DW is a system used in the database system where the data is stored in a structured form. There is a huge chunk of data collected from various functionalities of the business. This data is required to be stored by the business organizations in order to analyze it later for business strategy development.

The data stored in the DW is in a structured form so that in the case of analysis of the data, the required information can be collected in less amount of time. The DM approach is used for the purpose of analyzing the data stored in DWs and the database.

DM as the name suggests mines essential information form the large chunk of data present. This information is in terms of the financial report, business insights, etc. that help in the strategic development of the business.

The role of neural networks is very essential for the DM processes as the analytics is done by using neural network techniques that learn from the data and from the analysis report based on that. The essential neural networks such as feed forward and limited recurrent networks.

This chapter forms the analysis of DW and DM for distributed database architecture and their importance for business insights. A neural network is described in the chapter and its importance for DM has been provided. The OLTP and OLAP from the processing system for DW and DM.

REFERENCES

1. Adibhatla, B., (2018). *How Data Mining Works-Analytics India Magazine*. [online] Analytics India Magazine. Available at: https://analyticsindiamag.com/how-data-mining-works/ (accessed on 1 June 2020).
2. Berson, A., (n.d.). *Alex Berson Quotes (Author of Data Warehousing, Data Mining, and OLAP)*. [online] Goodreads.com. Available at: https://www.goodreads.com/author/quotes/272092.Alex_Berson (accessed on 1 June 2020).
3. Burnside, K., (2019). *The Disadvantages of a Data Warehouse*. [online] Smallbusiness.chron.com. Available at: https://smallbusiness.chron.com/disadvantages-data-warehouse-73584.html (accessed on 1 June 2020).
4. Data Warehouse Information Center, (2020). *Benefits of a Data Warehouse | Data Warehouse Information Center*. [online] Available at: https://datawarehouseinfo.com/data-warehouse/benefits-of-a-data-warehouse/ (accessed on 1 June 2020).
5. DataFlair, (2018). *Disadvantages of Data Mining-Data Mining Issues-DataFlair*. [online] Available at: https://data-flair.training/blogs/disadvantages-of-data-mining/ (accessed on 1 June 2020).
6. Dremio.com. (2020). *Data Warehouses Explained by Dremio*. [online] Available at: https://www.dremio.com/what-is-a-data-warehouse/ (accessed on 1 June 2020).
7. Educba, (2020). *Advantages of Data Mining | Complete Guide to Benefits of Data Mining*. [online] Available at: https://www.educba.com/advantages-of-data-mining/ (accessed on 1 June 2020).
8. Educba, (2020). *What is Data Mining? | Advantage and Working of Data Mining*. [online] Available at: https://www.educba.com/what-is-data-mining/ (accessed on 1 June 2020).
9. Guru99.com. (2020). *Data Mining Tutorial: Process, Techniques, Tools, EXAMPLES*. [online] Available at: https://www.guru99.com/data-mining-tutorial.html (accessed on 1 June 2020).
10. Kroeger, N., (2017). *Data Warehouse: Characteristics and Benefits-DZone Big Data*. [online] dzone.com. Available at: https://dzone.com/articles/data-warehouse-characteristics-and-benefits (accessed on 1 June 2020).

11. Lastnightstudy, (2020). *Data Mining Functionalities-Last Night Study*. [online] Available at: http://www.lastnightstudy.com/Show?id=37/Data-Mining-Functionalities (accessed on 1 June 2020).
12. Nagabhushana, S., (2006).*Data Warehousing OLAP and Data Mining*. New Age International.
13. Reddy, C., (2020). *Data Mining: Purpose, Characteristics, Benefits & Limitations-WiseStep*. [online] WiseStep. Available at: https://content.wisestep.com/data-mining-purpose-characteristics-benefits-limitations/ (accessed on 1 June 2020).
14. Tech Differences. (2016). *Difference between OLTP and OLAP (with Comparison Chart) - Tech Differences*. [online] Available at: https://techdifferences.com/difference-between-oltp-and-olap.html (accessed on 1 June 2020).

INDEX

A

abstract data types (ADTs) 128
access control list (ACL) 100
ad hoc query language 119, 120
Advanced Research Projects Agency Network (ARPANET) 78
American National Standards Institute (ANSI) 141
analytical database 204
Application system installation 150
artificial intelligence (AI) 50
audio clips 133
authentication system 23
automated teller machine (ATM) 48, 54
Autonomous technology 50

B

bandwidth 152
behavior analysis 205
binary relations 37
Bluetooth systems 70
Buffer management 121
business analysis 214
business communication 58
Business Intelligence (BI) 130
business network 58
business organization 176, 177, 178, 195
business strategy 205, 207, 228
Bus topology 60

C

Campus Area Network 75, 77
client machines 152
client security 165, 171
Client-server architecture 146, 147
Client-Server mode 131

client/server system (C/S system) 165
clients to servers 22
coaxial cable 62, 71
commercial systems 121
communication channel 157
communication protocol 147
compilers 11
Computer Aided Design 34
computer architectures 136
Computer networks 54, 56, 61, 81
computer system 20
computer-to-computer communication 66
concurrency management 129
corporate area network (CAN) 77
corporate network 71
Cost/Benefit analysis 217
cryptography 168

D

data analysis 204, 205, 216, 217
database administrator (DBA) 25
database environment 9, 11, 15
database security systems 21
database server 24, 25
Database services 160
database systems 2, 3, 6, 9
database tables 33, 41
database technologies 2
Database tuning (DT) 199
data communication 57, 65, 77
Data conversion 150
Data description languages 3
data dictionary 10, 21
data distribution 3
data encryption 147, 162, 166, 170
Data Encryption Standard (DES) 27
Data gathering 149
Data integration 210
data integration systems 87, 88, 98
data interpretation 177
data manipulation language (DML) 181
data mining (DM) 205
data organization 179, 185
Data security 99
data sharing 151, 161
data structures 3, 8
Data transmission 71
data transport mechanism 56
data warehouses (DW) 95
denial of service (DoS) 147
Department of Defense (DoD) 67
derived horizontal fragmentation 91, 93
digital versatile disc-read only memory (DVD-ROM) 72
directory service 24
directory services 65
Direct shared virtual memory (DSVM) 137
Discretionary access control (DAC) 99
distributed computing environment (DCE) 161
distributed database management system (DDBMS) 89
distributed database system 2, 5, 7
Distribution transparency 86
domain name 189
domain values 38, 39
Dynamic data exchange 160

E

e-commerce business 205
effective communication 55
Electronic communication 56

embeddable database designed 131
embedded database languages 11
Employee Management System 115
encrypted data 26
Enterprise Application Integration (EAI) 95
Enterprise Information Integration (EII) 95
Enterprise private network 75, 76
error messages 152
Establishing production environment 150
Ethernet cables 71
Extract-transform load (ETL) 95

F

Facebook 45
file servers 62
file system 184, 185, 186, 187, 188
financial report 220, 228
firewall 56, 64, 167, 171
Flat transactions model 104
foreign key 40, 42
Frequency distribution graphs 212

G

Gateway 64, 83
global-as-view (GAV) 97
global internet 80
global organizations 51
graphical interfaces 191
Graph structure 197

H

Hacking 69
hard-disks 72
hardware 2, 8
Heterogeneous Distributed System 7
home network 57, 58, 71
Homogeneous Distributed System 7
human resource 204, 218
Hybrid topology 61

I

Independent Architecture of Computing (ICA) 158
information management system 13
information system 2, 9
inheritance 117, 118, 119, 123, 126, 127, 128, 129, 133
Interface Definition Language (IDL) 141
internal database structure 222
internet 54, 56, 64, 66, 68, 70, 71, 72, 73, 74, 77, 78, 79, 80
Internet protocols 130
Internet Routing Protocol 77
Internet Service 64
Internetworking 77, 78

J

Java Database Connectivity (JDBC) 87
Java program 132
JavaScript 44, 45
JavaScript Object Notation (JSON) 123

L

least recently used (LRU) 137
LinkedIn 45
Local area network (LAN) 56
local-as-view (LAV) 97
local conceptual schemas (LCSs) 96

logical language 106

M

machine learning 50
marketing management 220
mathematical language 37
mediator systems 87
memory system 136, 137
mesh topology 59
Message services 160
messaging system 65
meta-data 7, 10
Metadata 178
Metropolitan Area Network 74
microwaves 62
multi-database systems (MDBMS) 89
multimedia film-on-demand (MOD) 134
multiprogramming environment 11
multiprotocol routing capabilities 65

N

national physical laboratory (NPL) 78
network authentications services 22
network bandwidth 133, 135
network cables 61
Network design 56
network interface controller (NIC) 76
network management 65
network model 139
Network Operating Systems 65
network security 57
network systems 12, 13
Network topology 57
neural network's 225
Not Only SQL (NoSQL) 123

O

Object Data Management Group (ODMG) 123, 141
Object linking and embedding (OLE) 160
object management process (OMP) 133
object-oriented database management system (OODBMS) 123, 126
object-oriented databases (OODB) 114
object-relational database management systems (ORDBMS) 133
object-relational mapping (ORM) 125
Object Request Broker (ORB) 141
online analytical processing (OLAP) 204
On-line Analytical Processing (OLAP) 95, 96
Open Database Connectivity (ODBC) 87
Open Software Foundation (OSF) 24
Open System Interconnection (OSI) 77
operating system 11, 21, 22, 24
Oracle database 49

P

parallel database systems 88
Password management 22
peer-to-peer (P2P) 57, 89
Personal area network 70
personal computer (PC) 80

personal digit assistant 70
Pictographs 212
polymorphism 126, 129
POSIX file systems 132
primary key 42, 43
Print services 160
Public Key Encryption 27
Python 125, 126, 130, 131

Q

query-based system 190
query by example (QBE) 194
query language 120, 128, 133

R

random numbers 169
relational algebra 37, 40
Relational Database Management System (RDBMS) 33
relational database system 194
relational data model 32, 33, 34, 36
relational model (RM) 12, 32
relational system 12
reliable system 28
Remote Authentication Dial-In User Service 23
Remote caching architecture (RCA) 137
remote computing 158
Remote desktop protocol (RDP) 158
Remote Memory Paging Systems 136
Remote procedure calls (RPCs) 24
Remote services 160
resource management 178, 204
ring topology 60, 61

S

schema management 86, 87
Secondary storage management 124
Secure Sockets Layer (SSL) 21
security management 69
servers to servers 22
set-theory 35
shopping pattern analysis 215
social security number 42
software 2, 7, 8, 13
software applications 61
software life cycle 13
Star topology 59
Storage Area Network 75, 76
structured query language (SQL) 37
Student Information System 115
System Area Network 75, 76

T

tables management 192
TCP/IP Model 66
Technology platform analysis 149
telecommunications 126
Telephone number 178
Three-dimensional diagrams 212
Time-series graphs 212
traditional file systems 182, 184, 185, 186
Traffic congestion 152
Train Reservation System 115
Transmission Control Protocol (TCP) 79
transmission medium 61
troubleshooting 61
Twitter 45

U

User Datagram Protocol (UDP) 79

V

version management 122
video clips 133
Virtual Area Network 75
virtual private networks (VPNs) 77

W

web applications 129
Web browser 64
Web pages 64
web services 130
websites 58, 81
WhatsApp 74
wide area networks (WANs) 58
wireless fidelity (Wi-Fi) 70
wireless media 54
Wireless Personal Area Network 70
World Wide Web 136